REGATTA

A CELEBRATION OF OARSMANSHIP

BY BENJAMIN IVRY

INTRODUCTION BY
STEPHEN KIESLING

Simon and Schuster
New York   London   Toronto   Sydney   Tokyo

A FRIEDMAN GROUP BOOK

Copyright © 1988 by Michael Friedman Publishing Group, Inc.

Published by Simon and Schuster
A Division of Simon & Schuster Inc.
Simon & Schuster Building
Rockefeller Center
1230 Avenue of the Americas
New York, New York 10020

SIMON AND SCHUSTER and colophon are registered trademarks of
Simon & Schuster Inc.

REGATTA: *A Celebration of Oarsmanship*
was prepared and produced by
Michael Friedman Publishing Group, Inc.
15 West 26th Street
New York, New York 10010

Designer: Robert W. Kosturko
Art Director: Mary Moriarty
Photo Editor: Christopher Bain
Production Manager: Karen L. Greenberg

1   3   5   7   9   10   8   6   4   2

Library of Congress Cataloging in Publication Data

Ivry, Benjamin.
Regatta: a celebration of oarsmanship.

"A Friedman Group book"—T.p. verso.
Bibliography: p.
Includes index.
1. Rowing—History.   I. Title.
GV791.I874   1988   797.1′23′09   87-32303
ISBN 0-671-64711-3

Typeset by BPE Graphics
Color separations by Hong Kong Scanner Craft Company Ltd.
Printed and bound in Hong Kong by Leefung-Asco Printers Ltd.

DEDICATION

To Joy, Amalia, Jacob, and GPF.

ACKNOWLEDGMENTS

The author would like to thank the United States Rowing Association for making back issues of its publication available. The staffs of the New York Public Library and the Philadelphia Maritime Museum were helpful, as were Stephen Kiesling, Seth Bauer, Matt Labine, Reed Rubin, Jennie Kiesling, and Christopher Dodd in offering expert advice. Finally, Karla Olson has been a tactful and able editor.

C O N T

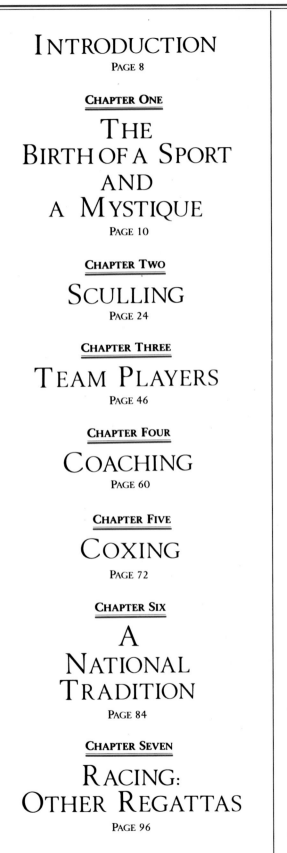

© Robert Visser 1988

© Robert Visser 1988

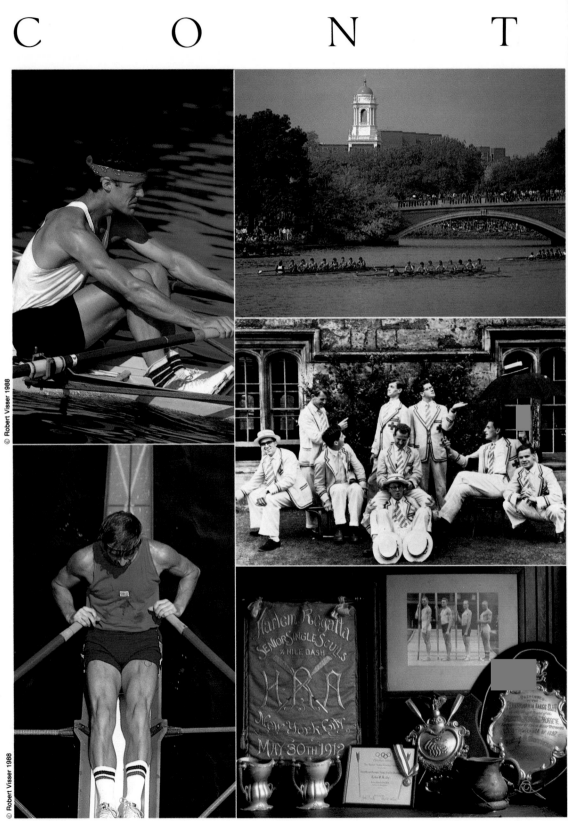

E N T S

© M.L. Thomas 1988

© Robert Visser 1988

INTRODUCTION

"Last" Rows

I don't know how many last rows I have had. There was my "last" practice on the Housatonic at the end of my senior year at Yale. It was only two days before my last Eastern Sprints so we were well rested and could relish the full glory of all those thousands of strokes of the early season without the fog of training fatigue. A few weeks later I rowed my last Harvard Race, the last time I figured that I could really believe we were putting our futures on the line in a boat race. A month later was my last row on an international team, racing in the finals at Henley on the Olympic team that never made it to Moscow. Then I retired. I would never again be so strong, I figured. My body would never again sing in the midst of such perfect harmony. The draw of the boathouse would fade with my muscles. I would move on.

A lot of us do manage to retire, at least for awhile. We move far enough from a boathouse or bury ourselves deeply enough into jobs or relationships that we can't possibly spare the time to get back on the water. But the sport does not let go so easily. For me, it was not just that my metaphors come from rowing, or that I size up people by where they might sit in a boat, or whether I'd want to be with them in the same boat. The sport was locked into my body. It took only a year of virtual abstinence before I bought an ergometer for my living room. Now, ten years later, I don't row much on the Housatonic—not more than once a year—but I fairly often find myself at odd hours on the Harlem. The long race against Harvard threatens to become an annual alumni event. I used to snicker when I saw men twice my age training for the Master's World Championships. Why didn't they grow up? I realize now that rowing is one of those special old friends who will welcome you back at any time and tell you something new and wonderful.

If there is any shame in rowing it is the tendency to be protective of our small community of men and women. Rowing faces no threat of commercialization. The sport is too difficult to learn, and it is what we learn from it that draws us together. We are an elite group, but not an elitist group, with a colorful heritage created by watermen and gentlemen, scholars and scoundrels.

By the time *Regatta* is published, one new oarsman, Benjamin Ivry, will have joined our ranks in a shell. He has already been in a canoe. He sat amidships on the bottom of the aluminum hull, wearing an orange, pillow-type lifepreserver, while my wife and I paddled at either end. A jock he is not—nor a true believer in rowing. Instead, Ben is a poet and an art historian. It often seems that Ben has read a book for every stroke I have rowed. His research for *Regatta* included several hundred volumes written in several languages. For those of us who see rowing as art of poetry or philosophy—as well as sport—*Regatta* is a fine addition to the bookshelf. I learned a lot, laughed a lot and came away with a refreshed love for the strange and wonderful sport of rowing.

Stephen Kiesling

9

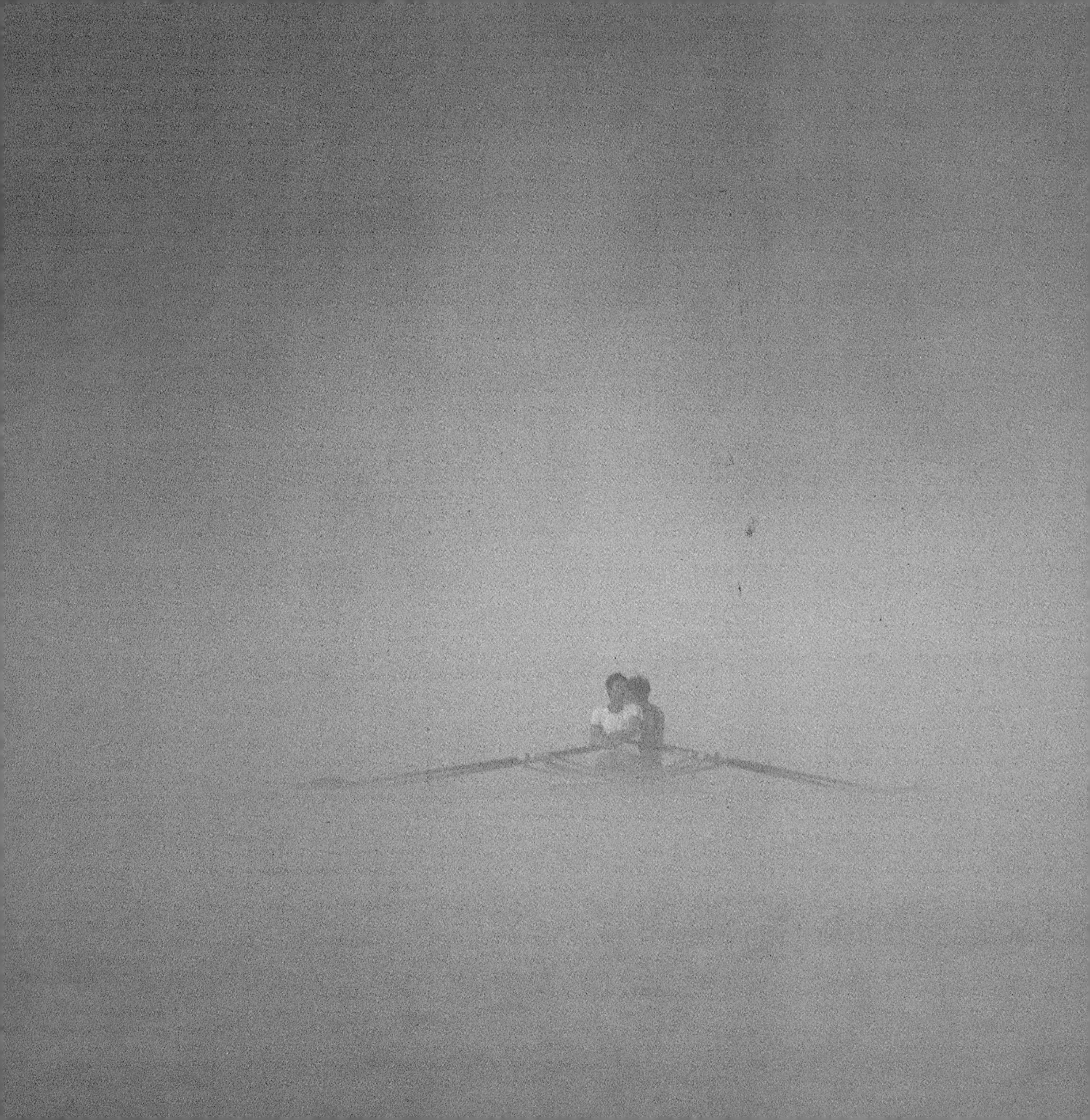

CHAPTER ONE

THE BIRTH OF A SPORT AND A MYSTIQUE

FOR THOUSANDS OF YEARS, IN EGYPT, Greece, and Venice, oarsmen pulled boats through the water, not as a form of entertainment and competition, but as a means of transportation. In Egyptian war vessels or Venetian military barges, the rower pulled with all his might, though the only appreciative audience was a sadistic slavedriver armed with a whip, whose primary concern was that the vessel reach its destination as quickly as possible. But even at that time no one could deny that rowing is fun to watch—a strenuous form of physical show that makes the viewer marvel at what the human body can do.

From its utilitarian roots, rowing has evolved slowly into the passionately followed spectator sport it is today. How rowing became a refined and glamorous activity is a fascinating tale.

Rowing has not advanced significantly in form since the days of galley slaves, yet the motivation and mystique of the activity certainly have. The British were the first to enjoy rowing as more than a practical endeavor. Three hundred years ago there were few bridges over the Thames River in London, and people who needed to cross hired a ferryman. Soon, gentlemen began to wager on which laborer could row fastest. Before long, impromptu boat races were staged for

FOR POET PAUL VALERY, water was a "source" to which a rower could always return to reacquaint himself with the nymphs of the river. In the poem "The River," he describes "leaning over a wide river, my sculls pull me infinitely, regretfully to laughing environs. Heavy-handed soul, weighted with oars—the sky must yield to the death-knell of slow blades."

© M. L. Thomas

entertainment's sake only. Testing the outer limits of boat speed was an eighteenth-century English obsession even before this time. In his diary for 18 May, 1661, Samuel Pepys, the English writer, described a boat race on the Thames: "Upon the start, the wager boats fell foul of one another, till at last one of them gives over, pretending foul play, and so the other rowed alone, and all our sport lost."

Rowing first became recognized in England as a ritualized spectacle with the unusual bequest of actor and playwright, Thomas Doggett. Doggett was a rough comedian, specializing in rustic characters with grotesque expressions; one critic described him as having a "farce in his face." In 1715, Doggett wrote in his will that a race was to be rowed on the first of August every year, "for ever." The grand prize would be Doggett's coat—a luxurious red garment— and a victory badge. His races began in 1716 and, with Handelian certainty, have continued "for ever and ever." The usual participants were ferrymen and laborers, but among the first spectators were Jonathan Swift, Joseph Addison, John Gay, Richard Steele, Alexander Pope, and George Friedrich Handel.

MORE THAN ANY OTHER SPORT,
rowing is filled with ritual, tradition, and aesthetics. The crew members hoist the shell over their heads as they carry it to the water, each accepting their share of the weight and the responsibility for the vessel. They understand teamwork even before they are on the water. At the end of a race, the losers hand over their shirts—and symbolically their identity—to the victors, a dramatic end to an almost always rigorous and passionate contest.

© M. L. Thomas

© Robert Visser

PAUL FUCHS (CENTER), SILVER MEDALIST IN THE 1986
National championships, strokes a quad for the New York Athletic Club.

Racing for a coat may seem an act of noble humility, but the vanity of British watermen must not be underestimated. Doggett's coat was a plush item, beyond the purse of the average laborer. To be seen strutting around in the garment was to be envied by all, bringing status well worth a strenuous effort. The concept of a coat as a prize grew in popularity. Soon, other coat races began, and this tradition developed into the modern practice of handing over the losing team's shirts to the winners of a race. The symbolic significance of the losers going barechested is not subtle. Without a shirt, the loser is stripped of his team identity. He is somewhat like the battle casualty of an ancient war, nude and shamed by anonymity. There is another "war trophies" suggestion in this exchange: Modern oarsmen might desire the opponents' scalps, but they must settle for their shirts. That these souvenirs are drenched with sweat is all the better; blood would be preferable, but is socially unacceptable.

For the victor, Doggett's Race was sweet indeed, an occasion to lord it over one's fellow rowers, as indicated by a Waterman's Song, preserved by the Fishmongers' Union:

> *I was the pride of all the Thames*
> *My name was Natty Jerry*
> *The best of smart and flashy dames*
> *I've carried in my wherry*
>
> *For then no mortal soul like me*
> *So merrily did jog it,*
> *I lov'd my wife, my friend, d'ye see*
> *And won the prize of Doggett.*
>
> *I Coat and Badge so neat and spruce*
> *I row'd all blithe and merry*
> *And every Waterman did use*
> *To call me Happy Jerry*

15

THIS PRINT REPRESENTS THE "GREAT
Five Mile Rowing Match for $4000 and the
Championship of America," held at Newburg
Bay, Hudson River, New York, on September 9,
1867. The gentleman on the right, whose fea-
tures are in rather terrifying focus, is the victor,
James Hammill.

In his will, Doggett specified that the race should be run on a stretch of the Thames notorious for its difficulty. Almost two centuries later, rower Guy Nickalls described just how trying these waters could be: "Never shall I forget the sight of six weary men in 1906 battling against a raging sea in Westminster reach, utterly unable now and again to scull at all, the boats full, their arms tired, missing the water mostly, or anyway stopping entirely every few seconds, to try and bear up under the strain of the huge sea, fairly smothering man and boat in mad turmoil."

Spectators endeavored to make things even more difficult for the rowers to add excitement to the race. For example, in 1736 a competitor was hit with a bottle thrown by an onlooker and nearly killed. Another favorite strategy was to hire large boats to crash into the opponents' boat during the course of the race.

The early oarsmen were built like boxing champs and rugby toughs, and the macho aspects of their contests were evident. In the 1782 race, it was reported that two oarsmen kept "pretty near abreast of each other till they came pretty nigh the goal, when the first man's skull split, which retarded him so such that the second man got in first."

This "pretty" instance of English understatement may explain why competitive rowing was seen largely as a suicidal jape for brutes. Pope, Swift, and other distinguished men attended the races in the same spirit that they visited madhouses and public executions, two other popular entertainments of the time.

The races whipped spectators into a frenzy of excitement; in 1754 members of a watching crowd attacked each other, and a dozen spectators were pushed into the water. Betting was so intense that men were oblivious to everything else. In 1795, a "thoughtless spectator of the rowing match on Mill Bank put a lighted pipe of tobacco into a hollow willow tree by the side of the bank which was not discovered until it was completely in fire and it was with great difficulty it could be cut down in time enough to prevent the fire communicating to other trees."

The contests grew in popularity, but always retained a flavor of the gladiator days. Rowing was still not considered a refined practice. The exertions of the sport could be deadly, and the watermen and spectators exulted in this peril. Only with an infusion of foreign stylishness was the sport transformed—an entire Venetian regatta was imported to London in 1775. This extraordinary happening was advertised as an entertainment that even ladies might enjoy. The term "regatta"—originally an Italian boat race held in the grand manner—was not new to the English. The pageantry and celebratory air of Venetian regattas had been noted by many British travelers. In 1652 a voyager attended a "costly and ostentatious triumph called a Regatto" on the Grand Canal. Then, with the cast of Venetians, the spectacle was brought to the British doorstep as "new Entertain-ment." While the display of military might lingered in the Italian events, in England the point was pure competition, or, as translator John Florio defined it, a "strife or contention or struggling for the maistrie."

The *Annual Register* of London chronicled the imported Venetian regatta, held on Friday, 23 June 1775. Part of the show was on the Thames and part was at Ranalagh, outside of London. There were so many "vessels of pleasure" on the water that a "gay evening was assured." Over 1200 flags were flown; grandstands were built to accommodate the huge crowds; boats were moored on the river to sell refreshments; and "bad liquor, with short measure, was plentifully retailed."

Maps of the regatta course were sold, and special songs were sung. One hundred "elegant ladies" graced a river barge that usually carried less visually appealing cargo. Alleyways near bridges were covered with gambling tables. Finally, the "wager boats" had their race, which was almost missed amid all the commotion. A formal dinner was served, at which more odes and ballads were sung, such as this anonymous song:

> *Ye Lords and ye ladies who form this gay throng,*
> *Be silent a moment, attend to our song!*
> *And while you suspend your fantastical round*
> *Come bless your sweet stars that you're none of you drown'd.*
> *Derry down.*
>
> *Enough of festinos, champetres enough,*
> *Bel-pares, and frescoes, and such worn-out stuff;*
> *But how to amuse ye?—Are there was the question,*
> *A Regatta was thought of—Oh lucky suggestion.*
>
> *From the lagunes of Venice we've stolen the hint*
> *And hope you'll acknowledge there's some merit in't.*
> *Nay we trust you'll pronounce it cool, useful, and hearty,*
> *As old Father Thames is made one of the party...*

The idea of rowing as a picturesque occasion was hereby introduced. The balladeers went on to describe the race itself:

> *Did you mind how each candidate tugg'd at the oar,*
> *How the managers storm'd, how the constables swore?*
> *Shall ye ever forget how the mob was delighted*
> *When the boats all ran foul, and the ladies were frighted?*
>
> *But the races are o'er, the procession is clos'd,*
> *The landing effected, the clamor compos'd;*
> *The fare that's before ye, we hope you'll agree,*
> *Is better than coffee, rolls, butter, and tea.*

And so the spectators fell ravenously upon the "otter-like feast" that had been prepared for them, introducing another custom—gluttony—to the regatta.

This extravaganza of 1775 was just the kind of marketing ploy that rowing needed. Instead of being seen as an extreme contest between laborers, rowing was now part of a pleasure pageant, a spectacle suitable for both ladies and gentlemen.

Of course there continued to be incidents of oarsmen being overstrained. In 1788, two rowing eights faced each other, starting at Westminster Bridge and finishing at Richmond. Bad weather hindered the rowers and the "exertions were so great after this encounter that one man may be said to have died on his oar and two others, on being landed at Kew, were taken very ill." Despite occurrances such as these, the pageantry of 1775 imbued the sport with a new level of audience.

Appearances and Reality

Over and over again, those who know rowing best have bemoaned the lack of visual excitement it offers the spectator. Rower and author Steve Kiesling has observed, "Crew is not exactly a spectator sport. Going out onto the river is something like going onto the dance floor." How can the excitement felt by the participants of a race be communicated? Compared to the times when rowing began, the world now has more sophisticated media, but rowers and fans have not been much more successful than past advocates in capturing the rowing experience visually.

Once the sport had acquired a popular following, some fans began to question how to depict it. Early rowing prints are noted for their unconsciously comic effects; the artists clearly had little idea of the mechanics of the activity. In the 1820s, racing eights were shown with nine oarsmen, and oars appeared on the wrong side of the boat, among other amusing errors. However, artists slowly learned the visual vocabulary for the new sport, and the challenge then became to effectively depict the effort involved in rowing—to show exertion. The engravers' solution was to draw the crews hunched over their oars in contorted positions, as if they were Ancient Mariners. The true form of the sport was sacrificed for drama.

Rowing prints were manufactured for the first Oxford-Cambridge Boat Race. The concept of sports portraiture was different then than it is now. A generic racing eight was drawn, to be labelled Oxford or Cambridge according to the print buyer's request. Later, the *Police Gazette* and other nineteenth-century sports periodicals featured many fine engravings of oarsmen, some with heroic force of line. Yet individual oarsmen were first truly portrayed by the nineteenth-century American artist Thomas Eakins.

The artist was a devoted oarsman, belonging to the high-toned Pennsylvania Barge Club. One of his childhood friends, Max

THIS PASTEL BY GARY KELLY WAS FEATURED ON THE cover of the March 1987 edition of The North American Review *(below). Thomas Eakins's masterpiece,* Max Schmitt in a Single Scull *(right), depicts Eakins's boyhood friend on the Schuykill river. Notice the other scull in the distance, which Eakins himself is rowing.*

Thomas Eakins, "Max Schmitt in a Single Scull," The Metropolitan Museum of Art, Purchase, Alfred N. Punnett Endowment Fund and George D. Pratt Gift, 1934.

Schmitt, was a great amateur racer, winner of the Schuylkill Navy's first two single scull events, in 1866 and 1867. *Max Schmitt and the Single Scull*, painted in 1871, now hangs in the Metropolitan Museum of Art in New York City. In this painting, Schmitt is in his scull, *Josie*, on the Schuylkill River above Gerard Avenue Bridge. In the middle distance Eakins depicts himself, rowing.

To prepare his many rowing paintings, Eakins made perspectival drawings, some as big as three feet by four feet (90 by 120 centimeters), which were bigger than the final works. These drawings were carefully annotated arithmetically, assuring that the rowing experience was precisely recorded. So eager was Eakins to show the sport accurately that, not wanting his signature to stand out obtrusively, he signed the canvas of Max Schmitt in perspective, his name fitting into the scene as if a detail of the landscape.

Eakins's work differed distinctly from the traditional rowing prints that showed oarsmen hunched over with effort. He submitted his study of Max Schmitt to his teacher, the painter Gerôme, in Paris. The young artist was proud of his achievement, but the crusty

19

old master took him down a few pegs. Gerôme admitted that the "person is well drawn, though the drawing lacks movement overall." He then stated the rules, as they had traditionally been adhered to, and how Eakins had broken them. His argument was that "two movements can be chosen by us painters, the two extreme phases of the action, be it leaning forward, with the oars behind, or leaning back, with the oars in front. You have taken an intermediate point, hence the immobility.... He is as if fixed on the water; he isn't leaning forward enough, that is to say, to the extreme limit of movement in that direction."

Eakins was surely aware that his work differed from previous depictions of rowing, though his teacher did not appreciate this break from tradition. The artist did not want to show his friend Max Schmitt in frenetic, undignified activity. To Eakins, Schmitt was a figure of iconic calm, a graceful balancer, a still denizen of Eakins's

Arcadia, where beautiful lean men went swimming lazily along river banks. Eakins's own presence in the canvas is a clue to the Aracadian homoerotic vocabulary the work consciously incorporates.

Eakins used the Biglen Brothers, professional oarsmen, as models even more often than he did Max Schmitt. While he was in his twenties, Eakins captured Barney and John Biglen in at least nine oil or watercolor paintings and six drawings—always depicted on a still, sunny afternoon, graced with a blue sky fleeced with one or two small clouds as a backdrop. When the Biglens won the first pair-oared race in America on May 20, 1872, the press reported them as "both dapper fellows, about medium height, well formed, and a very determined cast of countenance." To Eakins, the Biglens were larger than life, and he painted them in a grand manner.

Eakins also painted the Ward Brothers, four lanky New Yorkers who rowed a triumphant quad boat in the mid-nineteenth

EAKINS'S JOHN BIGLEN IN A SINGLE SCULL *(LEFT) CAP-tures the grace and aesthetic delicacy recognized in rowing. Edward Ives (below) and his brothers, Christopher and Michael, are perhaps today's Ward Brothers. Monopolizing on the almost ideal physique of the rower, they all began successful modeling careers while rowing in college.*

century and reigned supreme for about thirty years. The Wards fit Eakins's aesthetic ideal: they averaged six feet (183 centimeters) tall and 150 pounds (68 kilograms), with unbeatable muscular efficiency. A reporter described them in 1871: "They are long and lean and wiry, and when trained as fine as now, they are like greyhounds. Their reach with their long gaunt bodies and arms is something wonderful." A group photo of the brothers exists in which, bare-chested, they drape their arms limply around one another, striking premier-danseur poses.

These rowing pictures were the very first outdoor scenes that the artist painted. Some are masterpieces of American painting. *John Biglen in a Single Scull*, at the Yale Art Gallery, shows with quiet delicacy the way water drips off an oarsman's blade. Grace and gentleness compose the essence of these iconic portraits by Eakins.

Eakins developed his personal erotic mythology in the images he created of rowers. Rowing photographers have traditionally had more public concerns in their art. They have attempted to depict the excitement of the sport, with varying success, to a wide audience. Photos from the turn of the century often suffer from the aggravated stillness caused by the fine focus necessary to achieve a clear print. The result can be as static as Eakins's paintings, but without his emotional force.

The novelist Siegfried Lenz observed about rowing that "what is plastic in movement, withers quickly and is not good for photography." Yet if still photography presented challenges to the artist, moving pictures of rowing proved almost impossible. Thomi Keller, one of the least neutral Swiss men alive, is president of FISA, the international rowing federation. Known for his bellicose outbursts, Keller once spoke at a convention about how badly rowing has been televised. Keller noted that other sports, such as baseball, had changed their rules so as to be more visually effective on TV. However, this was not possible for rowing. He recalled a regatta in Chile in which rowers fought incessantly with one another, frequently crashed, and "nearly knocked oars over each other's heads." Keller observed that the spectators had a "hell of a lot of fun." He wryly concluded that rowing needs more of such melées to make it exciting to the television viewers who relish race car crashes, hockey brawls, and skiing tumbles.

As for commercial motion pictures, Hollywood early on attempted to embrace rowing, as in the Tyrone Power film *A Yank at Oxford* (1938), on which F. Scott Fitzgerald collaborated as a screenwriter. Leni Riefenstahl's documentary, *Triumph of the Will*, celebrated the bodies of German athletes at the 1936 Olympics in a sexual way that proved to be the wave of the future in rowing films. *Oxford Blues* (1984) was certainly one of the weakest of rowing films, but a star vehicle for actor Rob Lowe. More true to form is the historical film *The Boy in Blue* (1986), about the nineteenth-century

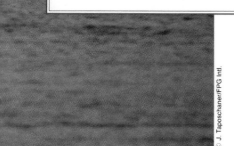

© J. Taposchaner/FPG Intl.

YOUNG NUN LONGS FOR FREEDOM ON THE OPEN SEA

*F*OR EARLY ROWING AFICIONADOS, THE SPORT *represented not only a fun pastime, but personal liberty as well. The medieval Portuguese poet Meedinho, who flourished in the thirteenth century, offered this verse in which a young nun bemoans the fact that she never learned how to row:*

I sit in San Simion's Nunnery
around me beat the giant waves
in wait for my lover.

Inside the nunnery, beside the altar
around me the giant waves
I wait for my lover.

Around me beat the giant waves
I have no oarsman, none to row me
in wait for my lover.

Around me open waves of sea
I have no oarsman, I cannot row
and so wait for my lover.

I have no oarsman, none to row
I shall die beautiful at sea's high tide
in wait for my lover.

I have no oarsman, I cannot row
I shall die beautiful on open sea
waiting for my lover.

Canadian oarsman, Ned Hanlan. The star of this picture, Nicolas Cage, looked as rangy as the average modern oarsman, although a slavish dedication to historical authenticity helped make this movie dull. Since a camera technique to effectively capture the feeling of rowing has not yet been devised, it may be premature to expect a great film about the sport. Yet Hollywood will no doubt continue to be drawn to exploiting the myth of the beautiful rower whether the excitement and challenge of the sport are adeptly captured or not.

The attraction of Hollywood to this myth is understandable. The image of the beautiful rower is as integral to American maritime legend as Herman Melville's "bonny sailor." As we have seen in the case of Eakins's models, some oarsmen were noted as much for their personal attractiveness as for their prowess. Some today are cashing in on the popularity of a rower's looks. Three brothers from New York, Michael, Christopher, and Edward Ives, began successful modelling careers while rowing in college. From the other side of the lens, fashion photographers such as Bruce Weber idealize the rower. Weber's 1984 Olympic portfolio for *Interview Magazine* devotes some pages to rowing. The women rowers are shown in realistic, unsentimental poses, laughing it up in a rowdy, unself-conscious way. By contrast, the male rowers are bathed in radiant light, caught with chins sticking out in dramatic poses, looking more like actors than athletes.

Poets of Rowing

Rowing has inspired a number of writers. Charles Dodgson, the Oxford mathematician better known as Lewis Carroll, first came up with the story of *Alice in Wonderland* while rowing with the little girl of his dreams, Alice Liddell. A third person in the boat recalled that with little Alice as coxswain, Dodgson called the narrative over his shoulder while he rowed. His friend finally asked him if he was making it up as he went along. Indeed he was, replied Dodgson, who continued to labor away as stroke.

The literary mind has also been unsettled by the exercise of rowing. E.M. Cioran, the Rumanian-born philosopher whose works have been brilliantly translated from the French by Richard Howard, is a case in point. It is better if some people stay away from boats, and Cioran, noted for his expressions of despair, is one of them. In his book, *Confessions and Curses* (1987), Cioran relates that while rowing on a pond in France, he became unnerved, crushed by the memory of a phrase from an English vocabulary lesson: "All is of no avail." This thought, in the midst of exercise, almost overwhelmed the philosopher. He conjectures: "If I'd been alone, I'd instantly have thrown myself into the water." Even in his earlier suicidal meditations, Cioran had never been so tempted to put an end to it all. Yet, it should be noted that Cioran is enjoying a vigorous old age, no doubt partly due to the fine exercise of rowing.

CHAPTER TWO

SCULLING

T HE SOLITARY ROWER AS AN IMAGE OF self-reliance has captured the public imagination more completely than other images of the sport. Alone on the river, becoming a part of the landscape, the sculler enjoys a sense of separation from the rest of the world. Daniel Topolski, coach of the Oxford crew, described the feeling in a memoir: "Some find inner calm and peace with yoga, poetry, or painting; I find it through spending a couple of hours daily sculling alone on the river. Only an afternoon of love-making can equal the delicious well-being and contentment it brings."

During a competition, the sculler is transformed from a solitary dreamer into a figure of single-minded application. Contemplation and refreshment are put aside in the effort to win the race. To this end, scullers train harder than any other rower: they know they have only themselves to rely upon when the day of the race arrives.

No matter how much time a sculler spends on the water, he or she is never completely alone. There are always other people to train with, and others whose expectations one must fulfill and whose involvement keeps one motivated: a coach or a parent, for instance. Two legendary sculling families of this century, the American Kellys

THE LIBERATION AND solitude of rowing were often used as a metaphor by the poet Anne Sexton, as in her poem, "Rowing:"

*I am rowing, I am rowing,
Though the oarlocks stick and
   are rusty,
But I am rowing, I
   am rowing . . .*

© M. L. Thomas

25

and the British Nickalls, illustrate the seriousness of some families' commitment to the sport.

A golden aura glows around the name Kelly, and not just in Philadelphia, the millionaire brickwork baron's hometown. The patriarch of the family, John Brendan "Jack" Kelly, born in 1889, was entranced with the world of the oar early in life. He recalled that he was always on the riverbank when he was not working. His greatest excitement was to "catch the oar or hold the sweater of one of the great oarsmen of the day." By age seventeen, Jack Kelly was rising every morning at six a.m. to row on the Schuylkill River (pronounced "Skoolk'l" in Philadelphia). He held down a job from seven a.m. until five p.m. and then he was back on the river until it was too dark to see. Every Sunday, his one day off, he rowed all day long. While serving in the army in World War I, he kept in shape by boxing, and he mentally prepared himself for a rowing career by imagining races with men he would someday have to beat.

When the war was over, Kelly's obsessive training paid off. He won the National Title in 1919. Soon afterward, an event out of American rowing mythology occurred. Jack Kelly planned to enter the Diamond Sculls at Henley, in England, and bought a new shell for this purpose. Just as he was about to depart for England, a telegram stopped him cold: ENTRY REJECTED. LETTER FOLLOWS. Kelly later recalled "reading that cable over and over, and seeing the tears drop on the paper, and realizing that all my castles were tumbling down about my ears." Kelly claimed he never received a promised follow-up letter from Henley, so he drew his own conclusion as to why he had been rejected: "I assumed the old rule that a man who worked with his hands could not compete was to blame." Kelly was frankly bitter: "As I looked through my tears, I felt my grandfather, who really hated the English, was right." His daughter, Grace, who later became first a famous Hollywood actress and then Princess of Monaco, often repeated this tale of how her father had been rejected because he "worked with his hands."

In fact, this story was false, and some sixteen years after the event, Jack Kelly admitted so in a newspaper interview. It was one of Henley's requirements that competitors not be manual laborers, presumably because they would have an unfair advantage against "gentlemen." However, the millionaire Kelly was gentleman enough for Henley. The real problem was a continuing disagreement between the Vesper Rowing Club of Philadelphia, of which Kelly was a member, and the Henley Stewards, the rule-making body of the race. They differed over what constituted "professionalism" in rowing.

This argument, indeed, had a long history. Professional rowing had flourished throughout the nineteenth century, affording great sums to oarsmen who were not above chicanery as bold as sawing the opponent's boat in two. Finally, in the interest of the sport, rowing went amateur with a vengeance, particularly in Britain, and to this day, there are stringent rules about a rower accepting money for the sport. In the 1920s, England looked with even less favor on clubs that offered some financial support to their members, and one of the well-known and repeated offenders was Philadelphia's Vesper Club. Regarded as a "semi-pro" outfit, Vesper was in bad graces with the Henley Stewards, and therefore so was Kelly. Kelly's rejection was not a class judgment, as he had told the story, but a statement about what the British perceived to be the proper nature of the sport.

The "honest laborer against the Brit snobs" story was a marvelous opportunity for Kelly to develop competitive rage. After the Henley ouster, he was like a man possessed. As soon as he could—at the 1920 Olympics at Antwerp—Kelly beat the winner of the very Diamond Sculls race where he had been refused admittance. Many saw Kelly's victory over the British champion of Henley as the honest American triumph over Brit upper-crustery, though this again was really a myth. The Henley champion, Jack Beresford, originally named Wiszniewski, was a first-generation immigrant from Poland, whose father made furniture for a living.

Jack Kelly's obsession to avenge the slight at Henley did not vanish with his Olympic victory in 1920. He trained so hard for Henley the next year that his fiancee "asked for waivers on me, as she couldn't compete with my boat. She treated me as if I had B.O." His sensitive fiancee finally forgave him his zealous dedication, and perspiration, and they married and produced a son, John B. "Kell" Kelly, Jr. When the child was born, his father vowed immediately that young Kell would vindicate the Henley Stewards rejection by triumphing where his father had been excluded. By the time he was seven, Kell was already working out in a mini-boat his dad kept for him in a mini-boathouse. Eventually Kell was the United States single sculls champion eight times, the best in the Diamond Sculls at Henley twice, and the 1956 Olympic bronze medalist. Afterwards, he served notably for many amateur rowing associations.

Kell achieved his father's ambitions for him, but at a significant personal cost. One family friend recalled that the young man was "right under his father's nose every minute." No doubt his father instilled in him constant pressure to win and a terror of losing. After one early loss, Kell's teammates had to pry his hands from the oars, so reluctant was he to face his father.

During the mid-1960s, Kell used the excuse that the "old man pushed the hell out of me" to explain some unusual developments in his private life. Having reached middle age, Kell was looked upon as a likely candidate for the mayoral race in Philadelphia, favored over the then lesser-known Frank Rizzo. But somehow at this time he chose to make the politically unwise move of leaving his wife and six children. Soon afterward, Kell was seen in the company of a prominent Philadelphia transsexual, Rachel Harlow, née Richard Finocchio, who owned an all-night disco where she performed as a

© John H. Shore

© M.L. Thomas

*JOHN B. KELLY, JR. (ABOVE AND RIGHT)
later in his rowing career, still participated in the
Head of the Charles. His political aspirations,
however, were dashed by his alliance with prominent Philadelphia transsexual, Rachel Harlow,
whom Truman Capote described as one of the
"swans of our century."*

A PRESIDENTIAL OARSMAN

TEDDY ROOSEVELT, DEVOTEE OF THE "VIGOR- ous life," was an avid oarsman at Harvard and later. In his autobiography, Roosevelt stated that he considered rowing a "great and permanent amusement." He much preferred rowing to power boating, explaining, "I suppose it sounds archaic, but I cannot help thinking that the people with motor boats miss a great deal. If they would only use oars or paddle themselves, they would get infinitely more benefit than by having their work done for them by gasoline."

Roosevelt went so far as to hire a "good-humored, stalwart professional oarsman" as his exercise coach when he was elected governor of New York State. He also installed a wrestling mat in his office. Unfortunately for Roosevelt, "the oarsman turned out to know very little about wrestling. He could not even take care of himself, not to speak of me. By the end of our second afternoon, one of his long ribs had been caved in and two of my short ribs badly damaged, and my left shoulder blade so nearly shoved out of place that it creaked."

go-go dancer. Rachel Harlow has been called "one of the swans of our century," along with Greta Garbo and Marlene Dietrich, by no less a judge of female beauty than Truman Capote, in his book, *Answered Prayers*. Worried politicos wondered aloud in posters: RACHEL HARLOW FOR FIRST LADY? Kell lost the mayoral race, but he served the cause of rowing well for the remainder of his life, until he died suddenly while jogging in 1985. His athletic achievements inspired many rowers, who wore "Kelly For Brickwork" T-shirts out of tribute to the great rowing family.

A strong contrast to the story of the Kellys is provided by the Nickalls family of Great Britain. Both Guy Nickalls and his son Gully were superb athletes, coaches, and spokesmen for rowing. Both wrote charming memoirs of their sport; Guy's was published by Faber and Faber, whose most famous author was T.S. Eliot, also a director for many years. The tensions between father and son in the Kelly family seem not to have been a problem for the Nickalls.

Guy Nickalls (1866-1935) is notable, among other things, for his amazing longevity as a rower. He won his last Olympic medal at age 42. As a beginner at turn-of-the-century Oxford, Guy was worked "almost beyond human endurance." Even when recuperating from a tonsillectomy, Nickalls's training schedule was rigorous. "After every short journey in the eight, and there were two every afternoon, I was forced to sprint round Christ Church walk swathed in sweaters." There was no chance to appeal to his trainers for mercy. The president of Oxford University Boat Club was a "terrible martinet to the new boys. No new blue was allowed to speak to an old blue unless first addressed. We were never left alone, we were harried from pillar to post, our rations of drink were terribly limited, we were marched like a lot of schoolboys to church every Sunday no matter what our religion."

Oarsmen were forced to go thirsty because it was believed they would thereby grow accustomed to the sensation. Dehydration was a small price to pay when preparing for victory. "No matter how uncomfortable you were in the boat," Nickalls writes, "how infernally badly you were rigged, no matter how deeply your oar dived, you were not allowed to make a complaint. If you complained, you never rowed again."

Despite this savage training, Guy developed a sense of humor about competition. In one race he was so plainly the victor that he did not wish to "show up" his opponent. So, Guy "eased up altogether in the last two minutes and . . . let him come right up level with me, and then, amidst tremendous excitement, put in four thick ones and crossed the line half a length to the good."

This little display of cat and mouse was but one instance of Guy's killer instinct, a necessary quality in a great sculler. On another occasion, he took a good look at his opponent before the race began: "I knew at once instinctively," he writes, "that it was a thousand

pounds to a gooseberry on myself." A friend later told him, "When you turned to have a look at him and I saw you smile, I knew his number was up."

Yet there were limits to Guy's thirst for victory. Once he defeated his own brother in a sculling contest, and he recalls, "It was the saddest victory I had ever achieved, and I wept like a child for half an hour afterwards and completely broke down in the dressing tent when my friends rushed in to congratulate me." At the highest level of sculling competition, defeat has some kinship with death. In his triumph over his own brother, Guy Nickalls had symbolically put him to death. So eagerly bloodthirsty he was not.

When Guy's son Gully Nickalls was growing up, his father was still enjoying his heyday as a rower. Nickalls Senior won at Henley in 1905, 1906, and 1907. Then, in a last hurrah, a crew of "old crocks," including Guy, was victorious in the 1908 Olympics. But, perhaps most laudable of all Guy's accomplishments was that he never forced his own ambitions on his son. Gully recalled, "My father, who was, I suppose, the most successful oarsman of all time, was very wise in his upbringing of his two sons. Obviously he was desperately keen that we should follow in his footsteps, yet he kept this to himself and never forced it upon us. Had we chosen some other form of sport, he would have been perfectly content."

Gully did, however, choose the sport of his father and was also an early beginner. At five or six he could hold an oar, and by age seven he was rowing. Recalling his first experience of rowing, he writes, "For the first time I took a stroke with all my power. It was a glorious sensation, the boat responded and sped on its way. Sheer ecstasy. Somehow I felt it was analogous to archery, and that the boat could be compared to an arrow as it flew towards the gold. I only knew that from that moment, insofar as was possible, I was determined to excel."

Excel he did, through self-motivation and a lot of hard work. Gully did not believe he had a natural talent for rowing, but that his improvement could only be achieved through labor and the "application of such brains as I possessed." The results of his hard work and determination were two silver medals in the Olympics of 1920 and 1928. As a sculler, Gully Nickalls felt that his most important personal attribute was stubbornness. "This, in many respects," he writes, "is an unattractive trait. It happens, however, to be a tremendous asset when it comes to any competitive activity."

For Gully, preparation and resolution helped him achieve not only prizes but also what he felt was the true joy of sculling, "that controlled and steady swing forward just before one takes a perfectly timed and instantaneous beginning with a powerful application of work—a thrust that sends the boat speeding through the water." Alone in his boat, Gully never felt solitary. The scull itself was his company. As he writes, "Sometimes it would seem almost as though

© Bruce Hands

the boat were a live thing, which, with its own particular brand of *joie de vivre*, was joining in the frolic by skidding along though the water of its own accord."

Compared to the Nickalls, today's great scullers often push themselves so grimly that they are labelled with the names of cartoon heroes, such as "Superman," "The Hammer," and "The Connoisseur of Pain." "Superman" would be the noble Finn, Pertti Karppinen, while Tiff Wood brings to mind "The Hammer," and John Biglow "The Connoisseur of Pain."

Six-foot, seven inches (two meters) tall, Karppinen is the winner of three consecutive gold medals in Olympic sculling from 1976 to 1984. He is a likely contender in the 1988 Olympic battle to dethrone defending champion, Thomas Lange of East Germany.

Karppinen is a family man with a young son, from a small town, population eighteen thousand, in central Finland. He works as a fireman, practices sculling, and consistently beats the opposition hollow. Reticent by nature, Karppinen seems to want only to give the world the unspoken message of his victories. After a phenomenal display of his art, Karppinen will murmur, "fantastic race," then disappear into the privacy of his family. He speaks only Finnish, which thwarts most English-language interviewers, and it is doubtful that he will ever write a chatty, anecdotal memoir like those of Guy Nickalls and his son.

"The Hammer" is the nickname of Tiff Wood won by the force of his stroke, which epitomizes power over form. Some spectators have worried that "The Hammer" will wear himself out,

ODE TO A SCULLER DEFUNCT

SCULLERS HAVE ALWAYS INSPIRED INTENSE DE-votion from their admirers. When the Australian Henry Searle, also known as "The Clarence Comet," died in 1889, many poets from Down Under emerged with well-intentioned elegies. These verses, dripping with grief, were duly published in The Tasmanian Mail _and_ The Brisbane Boomerang. _Scott Bennett has reprinted some of the most shatteringly memorable of these in his volume,_ The Clarence Comet _(Sydney University Press, 1973):_

> Upon the breeze
> A piteous moan.
> Re-echoes o'er our hills, our forest trees,
> In monotone,
> Are sadly whispering with baited breath,
> And every leaf
> Sighs deeply; for is not our champion's death
> A nation's Grief?
> From Grafton's stream across our land of gold
> To where the pearl
> Lies on its western shore, the bells have tolled
> In grief for Searle.

© M. L. Thomas

PERTTI KARPPINEN (PREVIOUS PAGE), winner of three consecutive Olympic gold medals, is perhaps the embodiment of the classic sculler. Reticent by nature, his obvious self-reliance and motivation are revealed on the river, while seldom discussed by him when he is off. His performance speaks for itself.

TIFF WOOD (LEFT AND RIGHT) HAS been characterized as "the personification of the amateur." Wood's single-minded pursuit of excellence makes him a fascinating example of the sculling psyche. Each morning he drags himself out of bed to face a cold, unsympathetic river and an agonizing, self-inflicted workout. With no crew behind him, he has only his own expectations to fulfill. If he fails to achieve his goal he has only himself to blame.

© Robert Visser

© Brian Hill

such is his punishing approach to oarsmanship. Tiff's training for the 1983 World Championship was so relentless that he broke a rib two weeks before the race. After five days' rest, Tiff and his rib made it through the trials. He explains with poetic cogency, "I am motivated by a sense of urgency."

Wood began rowing as a prep school student seeking social acceptance. He was not concerned with the finesse of the sport, not interested in developing the subtleties of the stroke. Such refinement is often not as valuable to the sculler as inner fortitude and concentration, and of these, Tiff Wood had plenty. Harry Parker, his coach at Harvard, later said, "I think it's really exciting that he's made it as a world-class sculler by dint of nothing but hard work and his own perseverance." In training, Tiff was motivated to the point that he

sometimes found improvement difficult to achieve. Parker once remarked that Tiff was "so interested in rowing hard that any attempt to get him to row better seemed to annoy him." Then, after hammering through the 1970s, Tiff finally learned some new tricks when a rival appeared on the horizon, the gifted sculler John Biglow. Under the pressure of Biglow's fresh talent, Tiff rethought his musclebound approach and captured a whole new string of successes in the 1980s, including the posts of captain of the 1980 United States Olympic team and of the 1983 Men's National team.

The title "Connoisseur of Pain" has been conferred upon Yale's John Biglow, earned by outstanding achievement in a career punctuated by injury. Biglow is a fascinating character, some of whose complexities have been explored by David Halberstam in his book

© M. L. Thomas

*IN SCULLING, A RACE IS USUALLY TWO
thousand meters (roughly a mile-and-a-quarter)
long, and it takes an average of seven minutes to
run. At the time of the 1984 Olympic trials,
Wood (left and above) had been training hard
for eight years, devoting an estimated 600 hours
a year. 4,800 hours of concentrated effort culmi-
nated in a crucial seven-minute-long race, which
he lost by only one second. One can imagine the
depth of his disappointment.*

DESPITE REPEATED INJURY, JOHN
Biglow (below and right) continued to train and compete at only his best level. Sculling is the perfect sport for a person of his determination and endurance. He can push himself to the limit without answering to anyone else.

© M. L. Thomas

© Dominik Keller

The Amateurs. A slim, stooped figure, Biglow might be typecast in a theater group as an elegant young butler. He is gifted with admirable form, sitting erect in the boat without artificiality. His determination to excel and his courtly attitude toward opponents, as well as the seriousness he brings to the rowing task, make him a chivalrous figure. However, Biglow is no Don Quixote; his antagonists are not windmills but flesh-and-blood champions, who pose a very real threat. In the face of challenge, Biglow never offers less than his best, an inspiring competitor to watch. His courage has won the plaudits of unsentimental rivals like Harvard coach Harry Parker, who praised Biglow's never-say-die attitude and his rowing savvy.

Throughout his career, Biglow has calibrated his body's response to pain with the objectivity of a medical researcher. At one point he rowed for some time with an undiagnosed herniated disc in his back. It is fitting that he decided to study medicine; Biglow's experience of bodily discomforts suggests that he will be an empathetic clinician. His stamina, ability to concentrate, and bedside manner should all contribute to his new career.

Most scullers do not have Biglow's determination, but at some point confront the limits of physical possibility. Because a sculler is responsible only to him or herself, overtraining is a common phenomenon. The overtraining syndrome has marred many out-

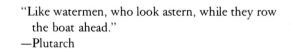

"Like watermen, who look astern, while they row
   the boat ahead."
—Plutarch

"Like rowers, who advance backward."
—Montaigne

"Like the watermen that row one way and look
   another."
—Sir Thomas Burton, *Anatomy of Melancholy*

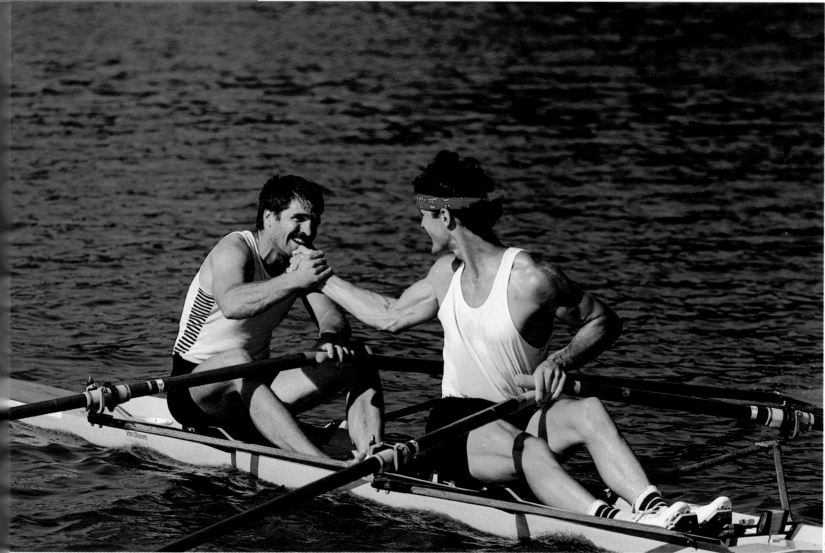

JOHN BIGLOW AND BRAD LEWIS
*(above) have rowed together successfully, but have
also competed against one another in the single
sculls.*

GINNY GILDER (LEFT AND RIGHT) *might empathize with the poet laureate of rowing, Paul Valery, whose poem, "On the Water," tells of "the calm, the calm and the magic ovals that make up the pearls falling from the oars."*

standing careers, such as Ginny Gilder's. Virginia "Ginny" Gilder, like Tiff Wood, never had a problem with motivation. Although she was fairly short and suffered from asthma, with a sustained effort she managed to make the Yale crew team in 1975, and later the 1980 Olympic team, which never got to Moscow. She won the bronze medal for sculling at the World Championships in 1983, and was, if anything, too primed for the 1984 Olympics. Her training schedule was relentless. Ginny rose at 5:45 a.m. in order to be rowing on the Charles River at 6:30. With a stop-off at her physical therapist's, she was at work by nine. In springtime, despite a full-time job, she managed to fit in an afternoon workout on the Charles as well. Then her body began to protest; an intercostal muscle was pulled and a rib gave way. Her injuries made her rethink her chances for the 1984 Olympic team. "I always wanted to be untouchable and I wasn't," she recalled later. "When I lost the first heat of the trials, I was hysterical, almost out of control." Ginny Gilder finally did, however, make the women's team eight, and she looked to rowing with seven other oarswomen as a "whole new challenge" instead of bemoaning

her lost sculling position. Happily, her crew won the gold medal.

Most rowing observers feel the current sculling star is Andy Sudduth. Sudduth fits the character profile of a great sculler to a tee. An introvert who works as a computer program analyst, he has said that he wishes he could row anonymously. For Sudduth, sculling is refreshingly devoid of ego.

Sudduth's recent competitive history points to a certain love-hate relationship with the event, but also highlights the passion and determination that is characteristic of most participants. In 1985, Karppinen won the World Championships, but Sudduth, taking the silver, gave the best performance of an American sculler since 1974. In 1986, however, he switched to sweep rowing and competed in the medal-winning eight, but in 1987 returned to the single and delivered a surprisingly poor performance. Yet in 1988 he trained intensively after a decision to remain with the single scull. His record-setting CRASH-B victory suggests that he is a worrisome contender in the Olympic battle between Sudduth, Karppinen, Lange, and Peter-Michel Kolbe of West Germany.

THE PYROTECHNICS OF THIS YOUNG TALENT, ANDY SUDDUTH (LEFT AND BELOW), *include a fire in his eye, a burning desire to win, a flaming talent, and a conflagration of opponents whenever he approaches the water.*

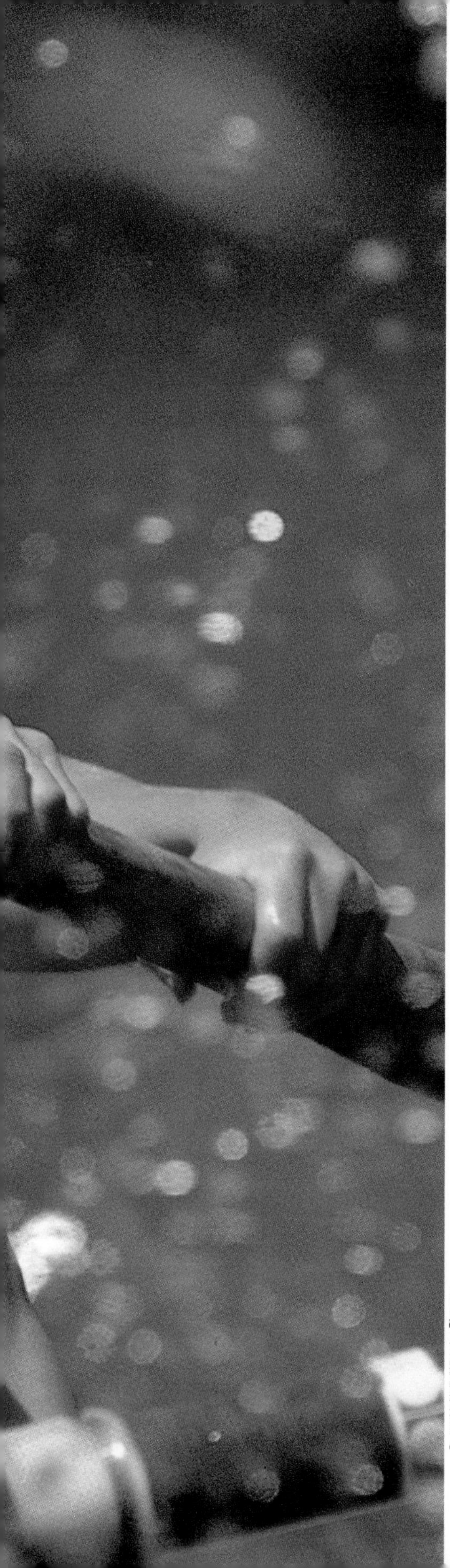
© Joe McNally/Wheeler Pictures

CHAPTER THREE

TEAM PLAYERS

THE EXPERT CREW IN ACTION IS A SPECTAcle aesthetic as well as athletic in its attraction. In 1970, when 75-year-old poet Mark Van Doren heard that the Columbia University lightweight crew wanted to name a shell after him, he wrote a four-line poem that evokes the synchronicity of a shell and crew. Van Doren compared the crew members' individual physiques with their racing shell, an Italian model, the Denoratico eight:

This Shell

Weightless in water, swift as the wind,
Subtle of purpose—a feather blown—
I go with my oarsmen where they will,
My beautiful body and theirs all one.

This verse printed on the sports page of *The New York Times* shortly after the dedication, captures the essence of a rowing crew's delicacy and streamlined speed.

The beauty of a crew's motion is achieved in a large part by an inner rhythm the teammates must share. The task of synchronizing

TO FOLLOW THE DROPS
sliding from a lifted oar,
Head up, while the rower
breathes, and the small
boat drifts
quietly shoreward...

***From* The Shape of the Fire,**
Theodore Roethke

IF THE ROWING COMMUNITY HAD ANY SAY ABOUT ASTRONOMICAL MATTERS,
*the constellation Gemini would be renamed in honor of a more recent set of twins, the Geers, Judy (below)
and Carlie (right), of Dartmouth, New Hampshire.*

oars can be laborious, and depends on a closeness and sympathy between each rower's body and those of his teammates. It is small wonder that in the pairs category, brothers and sisters, often twins, excel. The inherent empathy between family members is advantageous in an activity that requires such close bodily cooperation.

One of the notable pairs in recent competition is the Geer sisters, Judy and Carlie, of Dartmouth, New Hampshire. The Geers are able scullers, yet competing together offers emotional and physical satisfactions that other races do not. As Judy, the elder by five years, has said, "We're mutually bound to each other to do well." They have been doing well indeed; they were the United States Olympic pairs rowers in 1980.

To stay in competitive condition, the Geers thrive on health foods and practice concentration. They look at most other activities as an extension of rowing. Judy told *Sports Illustrated*, "Knitting is a lot like rowing. You do the same motion over and over . . . See, I like symmetry. In sculling and knitting, your hands are right here in the middle; you're perfectly balanced." Judy Geer has also spoken about the craft of rowing with gusto. "To row well," she says, "you have to relax between strokes; you have to wham it and relax, *wham* it and relax. Ideally, the recovery time should be longer than the time the blade is in the water. The thing about reaching out for another stroke is that you've got the boat going in one direction and here you are, going in the other direction. You have to kind of tiptoe up through the momentum so you don't slow the boat down."

The Geers appreciate the sensation of sharing their workouts, each sister a presence in the other's aspirations. They sit back and reflect on the blood blisters and calluses on their hands, and they remember rowing together.

The Geers and other women rowers have benefitted from developments during the seventies that gave women's crews a credibility they lacked before. Women have rowed throughout the history

© M. L. Thomas

THE TRIUMPHANT NAVY CREW (ABOVE RIGHT) MIGHT *have been inspired by the lines of Dr. Sydney Dangell, author of* **Odes and Idylls:** *"Pull thy oar, all hands, pull thy oar, till thou be stiff and red and sore..."*

of the sport, but often in the past people questioned how seriously. Many women rowers were recognized as achievers, but it was not until a team of rowers extended their unity and power to fight for their rights that they were taken seriously. For years, the Yale women's crew had been treated by the athletic directors and the University as second rate. For instance, women had no shower facilities, despite the passage in 1973 of Title IX, in which the Department of Health, Education, and Welfare required equal facilities for women's and men's athletic teams. For some time Yale and other schools ignored this law, responding to complaints from the women rowers with a chuckle, a sigh, and a condescending pat on the head. Despite this lack of support, the Yale women managed to place second and third in national championships in 1974 and 1975. By 1976, however, the nineteen varsity women had had enough. Together, they marched into the office of Joni Barnett,

© Gordon/Traub/Wheeler Pictures

Director of Physical Education, and stripped naked, revealing the words *TITLE IX* inscribed on their chest and backs in Yale-blue magic marker. Chris Ernst, captain of the crew, a senior from Wilmette, Illinois, read a three-hundred word statement, part of which read, "These are the bodies that Yale is exploiting. On a day like today, the ice melts and soaks through to meet the sweat that is soaking us from inside." Junior Anne Warner charged, "For four months Barnett has ignored our request for the zoning variance necessary to get electricity and hot water into the trailer and we'll probably get it when Peter Pan comes back to life."

However, the determined women did not have to wait that long. Just over a week later a zoning board of appeals in Derby, Connecticut, voted unanimously to let the Yale women use a fifty-foot (fifteen-meter) trailer for showers. The University, which had previously claimed there was no money for the women, announced that they would spend $250,000 to build a permanent locker room similar to the men's. The story attracted sensational press coverage, but the serious underlying purpose made the hijinks more than publicity hype.

As ringleader, Ernst noted that "Yale had lied to us for a couple of years, saying we could have facilities." Yet it was necessary to prod them into action with a "particular exercise in embarrassment for the institution." She reflected, "I don't think Yale would be where it is today if we hadn't stuck our necks and everything else out." It is a disappointment that not one of the rebellious rowers bothered to preserve a copy of the declaration that they read to Joni Barnett.

The Yale ecdysiasts inspired a 1980 Wisconsin women's crew to do the same. Coach Leroy "Crazy Legs" Hirsch, member of the Football Hall of Fame, was treated to a Wisconsin Badger rowers' striptease in protest of having to share a locker room with the male rowers. Eventually the Wisconsin women were given their own turf, and with further exuberance, the Badgers named their racing shell *"Né pret"* (Born ready) in response to the traditional race starter's query, *"Êtes-vous prêts?"* (Are you ready?).

One tragic incident in women's crew has been effective in establishing credibility among the skeptics of women's commitment to the sport. On March 18, 1977, Alice Platt, twenty years old, a National Championship crew member and a member of the Vesper Club for two years, drowned in the Schuylkill River outside Philadelphia. She was coaching a younger rower when her boat capsized and she was swept over a dam. This sad event served to direct the attention of fans and athletes to the dedication of many women rowers. The loss of Alice Platt was felt by the whole rowing community.

The Yale women crew's pioneering captain, Chris Ernst, in many ways epitomizes the team player. She has had an unusually long career as an oarswoman. She won a silver medal in the women's eight World Championships in 1975, and she has every intention of trying again for a medal in 1988. In between, she excelled as an Olympic spare in 1976 and 1984, and as a heavyweight double in the World Championships of 1985 and the gold medal lightweight double in the World Championships of 1986.

CHRIS ERNST (RIGHT) IS ONE OF THE MOST OUTSPOKEN rowers. She frankly refuses to contemplate going to Seoul, South Korea for the 1988 Olympics because she opposes the politics of the government of South Korea so strongly. Below, Chris works out with her longtime doubles partner, C.B. Sands.

At one regatta, a few World Championship judges falsely accused Ernst of taking steroids. Her reply, "Don't you know what someone who has worked out hard for ten years looks like?" quieted the protestors immediately.

A challenge in Chris's development as a rower has been mastering her nervous tension with relaxation exercises. Chris recalled in *Rowing Magazine*: "I used to be a complete mental wreck when I was racing. I came to relaxation techniques very late. When I got that under control it really made a difference in my rowing." She praises the United States Rowing Association for stressing that what is "really good about rowing is that it allows everybody to develop something special about themselves whether they're handicapped or weigh two hundred pounds, six-foot-seven and have all their limbs working. The very special thing about rowing is that it can help a wide spectrum of people enrich their lives."

Although Chris is still performing at a high level, she has no intention of trying out for the 1988 Olympics in Seoul, South Korea. She says, "I think the politics of the place are abominable . . . If I were to somehow be guaranteed a spot I wouldn't want to go to Korea." Few athletes have the conviction to give up a shot at an Olympic medal because of a clash of political ideology. Chris Ernst's rowing career proves that one can be a team player and an independent thinker at the same time.

The careers of Chris Ernst and others indicate that once the taste for rowing in a crew is acquired, it is rarely lost. One extraordinary example of an enthusiastic crew member is Dolly Driscoll of the 1946 Radcliffe crew that beat Harvard in an application of "brains over brawn." After graduation, Dr. Driscoll became professor of medical physics, specializing in cancer research. As her schedule became busier, crew was crowded out of her life. Then, when she was fifty years old, she fell down stairs and broke her neck and skull. Threatened with total paralysis, Driscoll was confined to a wheelchair. Seven years later she won the Women's Challenge Cup at the Philadelphia All-Disabled Regatta.

Driscoll was instrumental in setting up the Freedom of the River Regatta, Philadelphia's rowing event for the handicapped, and is currently involved in additional efforts to encourage the mentally disabled to row. Dashing about in a souped-up power wheelchair plastered with "Save-the-Whales" stickers, Driscoll has been described as an "old-fashioned sea captain." "She looks like Popeye," said one young rower. For Driscoll, part of the joy of crew is the experience of "using every muscle. There is also the competition, the camaraderie, and the aesthetics."

Just as the memory of victory in 1946 called Driscoll back to rowing, so do triumphs re-echo in the heads of many rowers, no matter how distant the contests. In 1983, members of the 1933 Kent School rowing team, all in their late sixties, reunited for a ceremonial row on the Housatonic River in Connecticut. Fifty years before they had won the Henley Royal Regatta Thames Challenge Cup, one of only two American schools to do so in Henley's history. That historic year they had also defeated teams from Harvard, Yale, Oxford, and Cambridge. In 1983, five of the original oarsmen and three substitutes took an old wooden shell out on the river. Their manager reported, "Gee, they still look pretty good." The crew members recalled how upon their return from England, their headmaster met them at the dock and burst into tears.

A briefer time span, though equally ardent affection, binds a group that calls itself the "Alte Achter," German for "Old Eight," a moniker they took because they won a silver medal in the otherwise tragic 1972 Munich Olympics. This American crew, mostly from Harvard, gathers every year at the Head of the Charles Regatta in

FIFTY YEARS AFTER THEIR GLORY DAYS AT HARVARD,
these barons of industry gathered in 1933 to show off their form. The septu-agenarians, who probably all detested FDR, show no evidence of demoral-ization by the Great Depression.

HAROLD FINNIGAN AS STROKE (LEFT) AND HIS BOATMATE
suggest that, at least in rowing, a body lasts as long as a gung ho spirit does.

IT OFFTEN BEGINS IN PREP SCHOOL

S OME GENERALIZATIONS MAY BE MADE ABOUT prep school rowers. They tend to be introverted. They are often near-sighted. Their physical coordination, or lack of it, disqualifies them from games that require a varied mix of physical responses. However, with all these deficiencies, they still find that rowing welcomes them with a hearty embrace.

The prep school rower garners not only acceptance from a team, but from the spectators of the sport. One such devoted fan was an Anglican clergyman, based in Hull, England about one hundred years ago. Dr. Sydney Dangell was the author of several books of verse. One, Odes and Idylls, *contains tributes to prep school rowers:*

> How thou dost move my heart, thou boyish rower
> as thy big boat the waves doth travel o'er.
> The blush upon thy cheek, fair as a girl's
> intensifies, as thy erect oar whirls.

Of course, most teen-age rowers just have a great time and grow up with fond memories, such as the comedian Lily Tomlin, who later became one of the United States Rowing Association's most generous donors. Or Alexander Agassiz, son of the legendary naturalist Louis Agassiz, who became addicted to the sport while rowing in prep school, and eventually refereed at Harvard College. Other high school oarsmen hit their peaks early. Former New York City mayor John V. Lindsay rowed ardently in high school, but in college he found he preferred blistering ears to developing blisters.

The point is not that high school rowers grow up to be famous people. Many of them don't continue competitive rowing past the age of eighteen. But, as a refuge from growing pains, rowing has served more than one adolescent. "Old boys" and "old girls" can still be seen gazing nostalgically upon a stretch of river where a prep school crew is hard at work.

Boston, with members coming from as far as California, Florida, and the Virgin Islands, and competes among the championship eights. The desire to row together is stronger than their sense of competition or their training. (In 1980, they placed twenty-ninth out of forty.) One of the crew states, "We're just happy to see each other. It's a very tight bond."

A similar tie unites those who took part in what some have called the most exciting crew race of modern times, the 1979 Harvard-Yale Boat Race. Coach Harry Parker of Harvard, not given to effusive public statements, told *American Rowing* that the 1979 contest was in his opinion "the finest race in that long series that I have seen and one of the greatest crew races of all time." Both crews were formidable and undefeated going into the Eastern Sprints Regatta. Yale defeated Harvard in the Sprints, establishing itself as the favorite in the Harvard-Yale Race. Adding to the Yale odds, the rowing stroke of the Yale boat for the 4-mile course was John Biglow, the talented World Championship sculler.

Yale drew out immediately to a one-length lead, but Harvard "held on tenaciously, responding to every Yale power ten [ten all-out strokes] with a power ten of their own," Parker related the event. "Finally, at the two-and-a-half mile mark, Harvard's power ten moved them back within three-quarters of a length. Biglow, still stroking at a punishing thirty-six strokes per minute, saw this and immediately drove harder to keep Harvard behind him. At three miles gone, he took another burst, stubbornly resisting the Harvard charge. But Harvard, sensing momentum swinging its way, drove even harder and began to draw even. With just three-quarters of a mile to go, and just as Harvard was about to draw even, Biglow squeezed another burst from his crew and retook the lead. Gardiner [the rowing stroke for Harvard] responded immediately and drove Harvard into the lead at the final half-mile flag." Despite a last-ditch effort by Biglow, the Yale crew was defeated by one-third of a length. Parker concludes: "The race was a magnificent duel between the two best crews in the country led by two extremely savvy and aggressive strokes."

In the 1979 Yale boat was an oarsman who has become a noted spokesman for his sport, Steve Kiesling. He is the author of *The Shell Game*, a book about what it was like rowing in the 1979 crew with Biglow and all the rest. Just as Harry Parker referred to the Harvard-Yale race as a "duel," Kiesling recounts that the night before the race, he had a nightmare in which he and his teammates duelled with pistols to the death. Kiesling's book succeeds because the author has felt the physical experiences he describes: "If the boat is really working perfectly, which is called 'swing,' you don't feel conscious of other people. You feel more conscious of your own strength through seven other people. When the boat goes perfectly, I feel it's because of me."

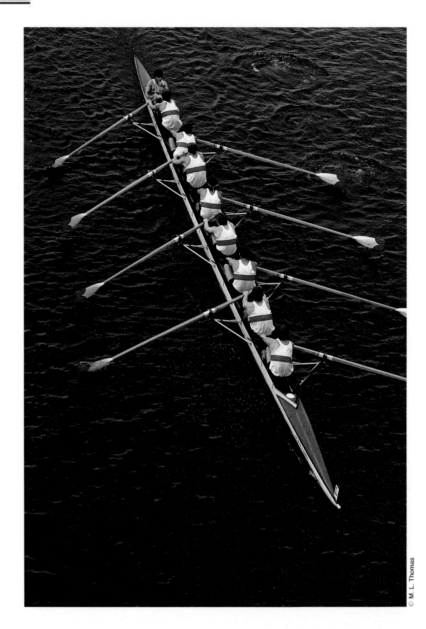

© M. L. Thomas

"You linger to see his back, and the back of his
   neck and shoulder-side...
The bending forward and backward of the
   rowers..."
—Walt Whitman, "I Sing the Body Electric"

As readers of *The Shell Game* know, Kiesling made the 1980 Olympic team, only to have the United States boycott of the Games keep him from the contest. He tried again for 1984, but this time, instead of fitting his training into the unencumbered life of a student, Kiesling had to juggle an office job in Manhattan and domestic life. He has not yet told the full story of his 1984 Olympic attempt, which failed by a hair, but he has described the hour-a-day training system he evolved with the help of a health researcher. The technique, called interval training, as advocated by Karl Adam and other coaches, saves time by alternating bursts of activity with rest intervals. While Steve's effort in 1984 was not successful, it indicates his enduring appetite for the competition of crew. It is an example of a strong team player returning to turf he knows well, the rowing eight.

Many of those who participated in the 1979 Yale-Harvard race were motivated to keep on rowing, yet few have attempted to describe the events in prose. In this Kiesling is exceptional, but the feelings he brought back from the race are shared by those who took part in the event. The eights contested each other with tenacity; individualists such as John Biglow submerged their egos in the common cause. The 1979 race epitomized the determination and stubbornness that motivates training for victory. One team lost, but both share the memory of that moment.

© M. L. Thomas

© M. L. Thomas

CHAPTER FOUR

COACHING

COACHING A CREW SEEMS TO APPEAL TO A specific type of person. Forget about the glory that coaches of other sports enjoy, let alone the public recognition or huge salaries. Those who aspire to mold a perfect racing eight do it out of personal obsession. Rowing and coaching are very different activities, with different personalities, and there are often sharp disagreements between coaches and rowers over what constitutes an ideal rowing stroke or the best training strategy. The history of rowing can be seen as a history of debates about the fundamentals of preparation for a regatta.

Coaches explain their training systems through various mediums. The coaches of Yale and Harvard, Tony Johnson and Harry Parker, respectively, have differed for years in their personal theories of preparation. Yet neither is a publicist for the sport or for his training strategies. Neither coach has written a book to try to convert others to his method or point of view. Each seems to feel that manufacturing a winning crew is the most convincing demonstration of an effective strategy. The result of their reticence is an aura of mystery about the two. This is particularly true of Harry Parker, who cultivates an air of inscrutability. A portrait of Parker by

RICK CLOTHIER, COACH for the Navy crew, addresses his able-bodied seamen. He might be repeating the Groucho Marx line, "Join the Navy and see the Army," as the Army crew will no doubt face these young men at some time during the rowing season.

HARRY PARKER (RIGHT), HARVARD'S COACH, COMES FROM *a distinguished line of great scullers. His mentor was Joe Burk, who, during the 1930s, was considered by some to be the greatest sculler ever. Parker himself achieved notably as a sculler, and for decades, as coach for Harvard. Vinnie Ventura (below) takes an easy ride while coaching for the New York Athletic Club.*

"Without me, where would you be? What would you do? Who would furnish you with food, clothing, education.... You have to sweat solidly over the rowing oar for that, and acquire, as they say, calluses on your hands!"
—Gustave Flaubert, *Madame Bovary*

HARRY PARKER (AS STROKE) IS AC-
companied by Charlie Butt, who is known in the
rowing world for having invented a kind of craft
known as the "Butt Boat." Needless to say, when
two such experts take to a pairs boat, their form
can hardly be less than admirable.

photographer Bruce Weber captures in Parker the eerie maritime resolution of Coleridge's Ancient Mariner.

Traditionally, European coaches have been more outspoken than Americans. The first truly controversial rowing coach was Steve Fairbairn, who began his lifelong association with the Cambridge crew in 1881. Before then, various Cambridge rowing authorities had published guides to oarsmanship, but Fairbairn's series of books, such as *Rowing Chats*, were different because he instilled them with all the personality that accompanied the dashing figure he was. A painting reproduced in his collected writings shows him wearing an over-sized scarf, with eyes that have the canny, hooded look of a falcon, a wrinkled face, and black hair.

Fairbairn's *Some Secrets of Successful Rowing* (1920) begins, "The object of this book is to get oarsmen to think for themselves." In Fairbairn's opinion, previous rowing authorities had overstressed the importance of upper-body movement, a leftover from the days before the moveable slide. Instead, Fairbairn said, the legs were a vital part of the stroke, which made "ideal form" in the arms and posture secondary to simply moving fast and powerfully. Smooth bladework was also one of the keys. "Orthodoxy" in the old style was out.

With all his wit and the novelty of his teachings, Fairbairn developed into a revered curmudgeon, whose words were influential. One of Fairbairn's most famous maxims was, "If you can't do it easily, you can't do it at all." This did not mean that his crews were expected to be natural racers. On the contrary, Fairbairn felt that "mileage makes champions." His idea was that a rower must practice hard and long until racing speeds come comfortably.

Fairbairn also believed that a rower must ignore forced postures dictated by "orthodox pundits." He stated that "oarsmen are not identically the same machine," that their body joints work in unique ways. He argued, therefore, that forcing all rowers into the same body pattern could not be successful, and that speed came from letting the rowers row as they felt comfortable. His rowing technique was to let the body work unconsciously and concentrate on moving the boat by working the oar. Instead of the traditional posture, with the arms rigid, Fairbairn advocated keeping them "elastic and alive." As a result, Fairbairn's rowers were accused of displaying bad form or no form at all. However, they won a great many races.

Fairbairn communicated his ideas through his books, as well as through his personality. By the 1920s, as stated in the anthology *Fairbairn on Rowing*, admirers were saying that "no other man ever impressed his personality on sport as Steve did on rowing." No coach ever inspired his disciples with such fanaticism, and "some of them seemed to worship him." Part of this following was due to his coaching manner. A student recalled his first view of the authority supervising a crew: "The familiar sounds of the river, the distant hoot of a tug's whistle, the hurried scuttling of a startled moorhen were

suddenly rent by a tremendous roar, "What the HELL are you doing, Four?" A meek little voice replied, "I'm turning the boat round." "No you're NOT," came the furious retort, "You're turning it OVER!"

However, Fairbairn's attitude toward teaching was the opposite of punitive. A nervous, easily depressed man, he found his worries disappeared on the water. On the river with a crew, he was happy. He said, "Every good outing is joy and every stroke is a joy in itself." Despite a life spent in competition, he felt that winning was secondary: "What does it matter so long as you enjoy your race and do your best?"

Fairbairn felt that rowers must be positively reinforced. Instead of pointing to faults, he stressed the goal to be reached. He tried to prevent rowers from expending energy on anxiety. Perhaps Fairbairn's own anxieties helped him to see the weaknesses of others.

The most memorable features of Steve Fairbairn's books are the snappy maxims:

> *Be delicate of touch; Remember that the boat is a 'she.'*
> *Don't worry about what you are doing, but think ahead.*
> *Trust to smooth, unconscious actions.*
> *Don't have sand in the bearings of the mind.*

He hoped that these slogans would lead a crew to recall the essential "Five K's: Keep quiet, cool, calm, and collected." He reiterated the illogic of stressing form above all else: "One wants to win, not to produce the most showy oarsmen"; "Handsome is as handsome does"; "Showiness is not always the evidence of usefulness"; and "If one sees eight men carrying a coffin, four of them with backs bent under the load and four turning their toes out like dancing masters, one knows who is carrying the coffin."

Fairbairn's theories spread as far as Japan, Germany, Australia, and America. However, his teachings were not unopposed. In 1905 a critic wrote, "Who is this Mahdi who comes from the other end of the world and preaches to us that our rowing is wrong?" Within living memory of the massacre of General Gordon at Khartoum, the title "Mahdi" was not a flattering one.

Before too many years, Fairbairn was dubbed the "Socrates of the Towpath." He relished his status and continued to turn out books of theory and maxims, some repetitious, and even sententious: "What an archbishop he would have made!" one undergraduate exclaimed upon meeting the coach.

Yet Fairbairn was aware of the limits of teaching rowing from the printed page, a medium even he deemed "very inadequate." It was better to show the beginners how to row, to let them see it, or, best of all, to put them into "a good crew and let them feel it." He disliked coaches who insisted on being critics. "Saying nothing is

YALE'S COACH, TONY JOHNSON (LEFT), is a rowing generation younger than his colleague Harry Parker, although prematurely gray hair has helped him win the respect and deference due a coach of his accomplishments. An Olympic rower himself, Johnson is inalterably tied to the sport.

© M. L. Thomas

often best" and "Coach the man to coach himself" were two of his favorite bylaws. As a result, though Fairbairn might say nothing to his crews, they would improve. Back at the boathouse, though, Fairbairn was more willing to chat about theories of rowing over a cup of tea.

After the worldwide success of Fairbairn's methods, some American colleges invited British rowing coaches to the States. In 1914, the sculler Guy Nickalls went to New Haven to serve as Yale's coach. Nickalls never verbalized a philosophy like Fairbairn did. Still, he left some observations on the sport. Nickalls's perceptions of

American ways included a critique of the town he lived in: "From a rowing point of view, New Haven was the worst situated place in America: an ill-protected harbor on which it always blew half a leg, and a small tidal waterway called the Quinnipiac River, which could only be navigated at low tide. There were no marked distances, the tide never ran two days alike, so that one could never tell if one's crew were really last or abominably slow." Nickalls was also appalled at the way the members of the Yale secret society, Skull and Bones, were "constantly attempting to interfere with my work; in offering unsolicited advice and in one hundred-and-one other ways trying to make it felt that Bones was the only thing of importance at Yale." Nickalls had never encountered such "constant persecution" by a fraternity, which he saw as a "standing menace to the American university system," a "caste society and liable to lead to sycophancy and snobbery in their acutest forms."

These factors contributed to Nickalls getting a slow start with the Yale crew. The impatient local press unleashed a "flood of vituperation" on the Brit. Nickalls, at the end of his tether, found these reporters to be "on the whole about the most ignorant men on aquatic matters that could be found anywhere." Fortunately the drawbacks of the landscape, the press, and Skull and Bones could not defeat a man of Nickalls's mettle. In 1914, he led Yale to its first victory over Harvard in seven years. Suddenly he was a hero, at least for the moment.

Overall, however, the Americans's experiments at importing coaches were failures. Englishmen like Nickalls found the never-ending squabbles over the Yankee teams' eligibility, along with endless grudges and ill-feeling between clubs to be "entirely maddening." After all, Nickalls and other Englishmen were brought up to regard rowing as a "piece of great fun."

Another of the few coaches to revolutionize the sport across continents was Karl Adam of Ratzenburg, West Germany. Born in 1912, Adam was not a rower himself, but a boxer. He took from fight workouts certain strategies, such as interval training, which, as explained before, alternates fast and slow segments of rowing. Ultimately, Adam's success as a coach was not measured by his innovative technique, but by his ability to build, from postwar disarray, a team that from 1960 to 1968 won two Olympic gold medals, two World Championships, and four European Championships.

Adam published a great many books and articles explaining just how he managed to develop such a victorious crew. His charisma controlled the sport in much of Western Europe, although how much his influence was consciously recognized in America is another matter. The Germans had, understandably, a more enthusiastic appreciation of Adam's importance.

Shortly after Adam's sudden death while jogging with his wife in 1976, a massive *Festschrift* was published, containing tributes to Adam and research articles that followed in the footsteps of Adam's training principles. A lengthy bibliography of Adam's published works was included, and a long poem by the noted German novelist Siegfried Lenz also appeared. Lenz addresses the late coach in this manner: "Who else has so keenly noted that every river has its opposing banks? Who else has, like you, amassed, fizzed over with the windowless knowledge between the start and finishing times?"

An assistant coach of Adam's contributed a long poetic meditation entitled, "Thoughts and Thanks after the Death of a Trainer."

He recalled the ritualistic playing of Beethoven's "Ode to Joy" after the German crew victories, and alluded to the boat races of Virgil's *Aeneid* in describing Adam's crews.

This tribute to Karl Adam proved that his teams' successes had a nationwide emotional significance. After more than a decade of destructiveness, Germans saw Karl Adam's training methods as helping to rebuild and create. Rowing was brought to the German consciousness in a serious way that has never been felt in America, and possibly not even in Britain.

One of the most passionate recent careerists in the coaching field is Polish emigré Kris Korzeniowski. After a somewhat free-wheeling beginning to his coaching calling in Poland, Korzeniowski defected to the West, through Italy, in 1972. In Italy, he worked at a variety of fancy sports clubs, where he says his time was spent, "flirting with the wives of club members, swimming, playing tennis, and driving around in the sports cars of young Italian brats." The Italian authorities eventually pursued him for working without a visa, while the Poles offered him work as a spy. Neither opportunity appealed to Korzeniowski, who opted for a plane to Canada.

Once in North America, Korzeniowski coached the Canadian women's national team, and later the U.S. women's team. In 1983, Korzeniowski took the helm of the men's sweep program, and today serves as the National Technical Advisor for the United States Rowing Association. His influence has been dramatic—under his guidance the U. S. men's eight has been the only team to win a medal in every World Championship since 1984, including their first gold in thirteen years in 1987.

The Pole's involvement, though successful, has also been controversial. From the beginning, Korzeniowski demanded a scientific year-round approach to training and team selection similar to the ascendant programs in Europe and the Eastern Bloc countries. He carefully chose the members of his team from a broad base of college and club crews, and drilled uniform technique and training regimens. His businesslike approach and seemingly coldhearted evaluation procedures ruffled wary American rowing traditionalists. When the system began to produce results, however, they became converts.

To outsiders, and sometimes even members of his own team, Korzeniowski can seem cold and merciless. But there is little disagreement that he is one of the most knowledgeable, effective, and respected coaches in the world. By his own admission, Korzeniowski is a dichotomy—extremely driven, but underneath it all, very emotional. "When I am coaching," he says, "nothing else matters." When his men's eight impressively won their first heat at the World Championships in 1987, however, Korzeniowski was in tears. Even his most vocal critics have found that this perfectionist has a heart.

Across the ocean in Britain, Daniel Topolski, coach of Oxford's crew, matches Korzeniowski's flair. In addition to being a coach,

KRIS KORZENIOWSKI (PREVIOUS PAGE), NOW COACH OF
the U.S. Olympic Team, is a difficult man to please, but he has been getting undeniable results in recent competitions. His sometimes dour demeanor is lightened by a good sense of humor, however. For example, his calisthenic routine incorporates an element of play. The rowers hop about, pulling each other by the leg Keystone Cops style. The exercise provides good conditioning and lifts team morale.

DAN TOPOLSKI (BELOW), OXFORD'S FORMER COACH, IS
here seen in a launch with Prince Rainier of Monaco (left) and the late Princess Grace (middle). Her Serene Highness is seeking protection from the cold wind, not hiding from paparazzi.

© John H. Shore

COACH LIZ O'LEARY (BELOW) HAS LONG BEEN A MAINSTAY
of the rowing effort at Radcliffe, where she inspires the women athletes with
a seriousness of purpose.

Topolski is a freelance journalist, photographer, and traveller. His father is the Anglo-Polish painter Feliks Topolski. This cosmopolitan background contributes to Topolski's skilled manipulation of his crew: he has dealt with obnoxious Americans, relating their insults with pride in his memoir, *Boat Race: The Oxford Revival.* He carefully recorded American Dave Sawyier's statement to him after a race: "You've never coached anything before and you've only rowed in dogshit crews. You don't know anything…This crew is pussy." Topolski seems to be able to absorb personal abuse with the gusto of Lawrence of Arabia, an English stoicism that few American coaches could match.

According to Topolski, when he trains his crews, he has them run races until they are screaming at him in rage, "You fucking bastard, I'll show you, you shitface." The emotionalism of Topolski's training methods can definitely pay off; his crews have a consistent winning record. Yet the charged atmosphere before races can take a toll on the more sensitive oarsmen.

One of Topolski's best collaborations was with oarsman Boris Rankov, the only man to row in six Oxford-Cambridge Boat Races. After practices, Rankov would be seen standing beside one of Oxford's buildings, beating a wall with his fist and groaning in despair, "This is the worst day of my life!" Races were equally emotional for Rankov. After the 1977 Oxford-Cambridge Boat Race, Rankov spent a week in bed. As he recalls the experience, "I couldn't focus my eyes properly for five days."

Topolski motivates his team's workouts with a combination of praise and blame. After the team's 1979 victory, he kissed each of the rowers individually. His passionate advocacy of rowing convinces even recalcitrant oarsmen: "The comradeship of teamwork, the joint effort producing an almost mystical intimacy when everything is clicking together perfectly. That unity is almost sexual in its intensity and one forgives one's crewmates everything, all their annoying little quirks and habits, for those moments of bliss."

Yet Topolski's pep-talks can have a sadistic slant: "Going into the final pre-race talk one year, I wanted to give them a sense of turning the screw on Cambridge at a critical moment and I suggested that each man imagine he was holding the balls of his opposite number in his hand and that he was squeezing them tighter and tighter as the race progressed. The trouble was, we were being filmed for a BBC documentary at the time, and their faces showed a lovely array of reactions." As a voice for the competitive passion of crews, Topolski is a coach with few equals.

James Ten Eyck, an outstanding American oarsman and coach, once said, "I can teach a man to row, but I can't teach him not to quit." Karl Adam, Steve Fairbairn, Kris Korzeniowski, Daniel Topolski, and a handful of other coaches were able to do both.

CHAPTER FIVE

COXING

OXSWAIN IS ONE OF THOSE FASCINATING words as old as the English language. It comes from the fusion of the Middle English "cox/cock," which means small boat, and "swain," which means servant. Yet to say that a coxswain is a "servant of the small boat" does not explain the term. The root "cox" or "coq" derives from the Latin "caudex," the tree trunk from which such vessels were carved. Swain, apart from servant, also means a country gallant. Imagine a wily, sharp-tongued, gimlet-eyed rustic aboard a narrow unsteady boat, and you have captured an accurate etymological sense of the word "coxswain." Today, the word refers to the steerer of a racing shell. Spelling reformers have argued that the word should be written "coxwain," as the "s" and "x" in the current form are redundant. Most people today shorten the word to "cox" anyway.

On the water, the crew is safe from a coach's excoriating comments. Yet they face instead, with every stroke, another taskmaster in the cox. A miniature version of the coach, the cox derides the oarsmen with glee, demanding more than they can give, grilling them that they have a responsibility to win the race. It is no wonder that coxes are treated with the disgruntled familiarity of an annoying

THE COXSWAIN IS THE only person in the boat who can see where the team is headed. He steers the boat and keeps an eye out for any obstacles. He also informs the team of the progress of the competition, then tells them how to win the race. Like a miniature coach, the cox keeps on the rowers' backs, pushing them to the limits of their endurance. Yet he must be careful not to push them too far; after all, he is getting a free ride from his hardworking teammates.

© M. L. Thomas

THE TRADITIONAL MANHANDLING OF THE COX BY THE rest of the crew after a victory is a ritual most spectators—and most rowers— relish. They enjoy seeing the little big mouth rewarded for the incessant yapping that led to the win.

© M. L. Thomas

brother or sister. The comedian Dudley Moore, famous for his short stature, was asked why he never coxed for his alma mater, Magdalen College, Oxford. In reply he provided a capsule view of the coxing life: "If you win, you get tossed into the water. If you lose, you get beaten up at three a.m. by eight burly blokes." The ritual of the winning team tossing their cox into the water will probably never change. The spectacle satisfies the crew and spectators, who resent this powerful person who appears to get a free ride.

The cox is, however, an essential part of any crew. He or she steers the vessel with a rudder device that is the size of a credit card. The cox must direct the crew down the course, and no matter how sharp-eyed he or she is, it is always difficult to see past the broad shoulders of the rowers. Before the race, the cox carefully studies the quirks of each stretch of river. Like a river pilot in the old days of the Mississippi did, the cox navigates, though his commands are rather different from the ferryboat captain's "Mark twain." The cox tells the crew whether they are losing or winning and by how much: "I have six seats, seven seats." He or she decides when to demand a series of strokes to advance the boat: "Now a power ten." These commands are carefully timed, and more motivating than the constant "stroke, stroke, stroke" of the cliché.

The cox is like the prompter at the opera, who sits in a box onstage and utters the text to the singers who are in the spotlight. Unlike a prompter, however, the cox composes a new opera with every race. The rowers must be dexterous enough to accept the cox's commands and translate them into action. The cox must be a subtle psychologist and win the participants' respect by addressing them in the manner that guarantees best results. Some rowers need to be screamed at; others prefer a polite murmur. Most coxes wear microphones, which allows them to use volume strategically. They can convey subtle instructions to the crew, then turn the sound up, and broadside insults to opponents.

Coxes are known to get carried away. At the 1928 Olympics in Amsterdam, the gold medal United States crew was coxed by Don Blessing of Berkeley. *The New York Times* reported that Blessing gave "one of the greatest performances of demoniacal howling ever heard on a terrestrial planet . . . He gave the impression of a terrier suddenly gone mad. But such language and what a vocabulary! One closed one's eyes and waited for the crack of a final cruel whip across the backs of the galley slaves." There are two points in defense of Don Blessing. First, these were the days before microphones, so lung power was needed to be heard over the water. Second, and more importantly, Blessing's team got the gold. Nowadays, most coxes are more restrained, because few rowers would respond to the galley slave approach, to put it mildly.

An important introduction into men's crews has been the use of women coxes. In 1972, a University of Oregon student named

© Bruce Hands

© M. L. Thomas

ENVIED BY SPECTATORS BECAUSE THEY SEEM TO BE GET- *ting a free ride, coxswains tend to be abused. When they are admired, it is usually not the kind of plaudits they hope for. For example, the British novelist Frederick Rolfe, Baron Corvo, who wrote in 1910 (Venice Letters) about an Italian cox he met in Venice, Zorzi, a "slight little fellow of 17 who steered the Bucintoro eight to victory at the Olympic Games at Athens two years ago." However, Rolfe's admiration does not focus on Zorzi's skill as a coxswain, but rather on "such soft smooth flesh! Such a delicate rounded form, strong and subtle."*

Just look at him peering, as sharp as a rat
From under his rum little shaggy black hat.
—Sir George Trevelyan, "The Coxswain"

Vicky Brown became the cox of the Oregon Webfoot crew. The press reported the story with an arch coyness that by 1972 was probably only permissible in the sports pages. The Oregon coach noted condescendingly that "girls are not eligible to compete in men's sports," according to the NCAA.

Vicky Brown faced difficulties, but two years later a larger and more staunchly sexist obstacle came to the fore. Mimi Sherman, cox of the Santa Clara University heavyweight men's crew paid her own airfare to Great Britain to compete in the Henley Regatta. Upon her arrival, she found that the Henley Stewards forbade "the pig-tailed Californian"—as the papers described her—to compete. They could point to no specific rule that banned women, but announced with finality, "It would be against the tradition of Henley."

By the early eighties, attitudes toward women in rowing had relaxed to the point that a woman cox was merely a spicy item for the tabloids. Susan Brown, an undergraduate at Oxford, had some success as a cox for the men's crew, and for a time was given almost as much photo coverage as Princess Di.

Oxford coach Daniel Topolski reacted in a typical manner to the participation of Brown. "It was difficult," he wrote, "to sweat and spit and fart and swear, as an oarsman does in mid-effort, with a diminutive, prim little lady perched a foot from your nose." The Oxford crew accepted Brown as a teammate, not as a "little lady." When the British press photographers became too ardent in their pursuit of her, the other members of the crew defended her with, "Sod off, you vultures, and go back to Lady Di."

One of the earliest traditions of crew was the practice of taking a lightweight child on board as cox. The youngest gold medalist in Olympic history was a French boy, about nine years old, who coxed the winning Dutch pair in 1900. He was recruited at the last moment after the scheduled Dutch cox weighed in a bit too heavy. After his ousting, the Dutch cox avenged himself by taking the four-boat to a silver medal and the eight to a bronze. His name is remembered, while the French boy is described as "unknown" in all record books.

Over the years, other youthful Olympic coxes have included 12-year-old Noel Vandernotte of the bronze medal French pair of 1936. Pairs rowing is a domain for a young cox, as the oarsmen can become so rhythmically adjusted to each other's style that a cox is not vital as strategist. Instead of a substitute coach, the rowers simply need a light body to steer and point out obstacles.

At the 1984 Olympics in Los Angeles, the Belgian pairs team had a 12-year-old cox, Philippe Cuellenaere, who described the whole experience as *"fantastique."* With his time unencumbered by a job, Philippe had always been available when the oarsmen were practicing. When they made it to the Olympics, they felt they should include him. One of the rowing Belgians confided, "Philippe is not always great in practice but we have noticed that he does better in

THOSE WHO LACK DUE RESPECT FOR COXSWAINS SHOULD remember that among their number was the young Emperor Hirohito of Japan, who, until 1945, was a "divine being." Since the rest of the people in a boat have always been mere mortals, some of Hirohito's aura, not to mention his courtesy, has probably been passed on to those who cox today.

© Robert Visser

competition." The press dutifully picked up the story of Philippe, reporting that his favorite foods in the Olympic Village restaurant were "cornflakes and yoghurt." Despite this hoopla, the Belgians did not secure a medal in 1984.

Lightweight adults, children, where will the quest for the skinny coxswain end? For a while 130-pound (60 kilograms) men starved themselves below 100 pounds (45 kilograms) to prove their devotion to the crew. Women as light as 80 pounds (36 kilograms) were drafted for the cause. There were many piteous scenes in college dining halls, as coxes watched the rowers consume their massive

meals then savored their own stalks of celery. Anorexia threatened more than one cox, until, in 1982, the Rowing Association fixed a minimum requirement of 50 kilograms (110 pounds) for male coxes and 45 kilograms (99 pounds) for women. Coxes are now slim within reason, and no longer find it necessary to starve themselves.

Coxing requires lightness, mental alertness, good eyesight and judgment, steadiness, balance, and a degree of manual dexterity, but it does not require mobility, and handicapped athletes have been successful coxes. In Britain, a Cambridge student, John Willis, who had no legs and no arms past the elbow, coxed boats to victory on the

© M. L. Thomas

Cam. His involvement with the sport began with a fellow student's ironic witticism: "Someone as a joke suggested that I start coxing as I was so light. I went down to the boathouse to try to steer a four and didn't hit a bank, so they put me in a novice boat and I have been on the River every term since." Wearing a leather harness attached to the rudder strings, he steered the boat by moving his shoulders. Built more squarely than most coxes, Willis found he added stability to boat's stern. He was dependent on friends to take him from his wheelchair to the boat, but he gained a sense of independence on the water: "This is the first time in my life that I have been able to compete on an equal basis, which is why I enjoy it. If I take corners badly, then people criticize me, but not because of my disability."

Duke University also had a handicapped cox, Derek Ward-Thompson, a student of physics who was born without arms. What happens if these people fall into the water? There is an element of danger when any rower hits the water, but the ability to float is more important than being a strong swimmer. Any person overboard should be able to stay afloat until someone comes to the rescue.

One of the more articulate coxes is Seth Bauer, cox of the United States gold-medal 1987 Olympic team and a freelance writer in Boston. Bauer has written some reflections on the art of coxing and has also participated in an instructional video entitled *Power Ten: The Rowing Machine Companion*. This tape includes a sequence showing Bauer coxing an eight on a practice run on the

Charles River. The viewer sees only the back of the talented oarsman Charlie Altekruse and the passing scenery, while Bauer is heard offscreen. The overwhelming impression of the sequence is that the cox is in command. Bauer sets the speed of the strokes for the practice, and tells the crew, "Ready all, row." The commands that follow are chanted in a subtle rhythm that is sympathetic to athletic endeavor, as if the cox is part of the athlete's body. No sooner have the oarsmen begun rowing than Bauer announces, "Okay, all warmed up. Ready to lay into a piece." There is no disagreement from the rowers. Bauer continues, "Four minutes. Gonna fill the riggings in a piece." His words blend naturally with the splash of the oars on the water. The voice is no louder than it has to be, a light baritone with a kind tone. It is as if the cox is charming the large oarsmen to do as he says, passing along his instructions with the rhythm of the stroke speed.

A good cox understands the importance of balance and speaks with the crew rather than against them. Within the great strength that is the essence of the pull of the oar, rower's movements follow a precise and deliberate rhythm. If a sudden rudeness of tone interjects and opposes this rhythm, the boat can be upset and momentum broken. Bauer as cox pursues a steady, supportive tone in delivering his commands.

In his video-taped practice, as Bauer increases the number of strokes per minute, the oars, looking like tremendous pencils, propel the boat forward so that it dramatically gains speed. Bauer adds with relish, "All the way into the body, please. Steady at the tracks. Yeah, that's what we're looking for." The polite "please" helps to make the crew work.

Almost immediately, Bauer decides to speed up again: "We're going to up in two, on this one, we're going up. Put your legs down now." The tone is triumphant, an articulation of faith in the athlete's abilities: "How much wood can you get out of the boat? How much send can you get? Squeeze on through. Yes!"

Bauer continues to call the ratings up, with a combination of praise and subtle persuasion that makes the rowers feel good about themselves individually and as a team. He calls for power ten, ten strong strokes to propel the boat at full speed: "Yeah, test it on the legs, let's take ten for the legs right here, on this one, stroke!" The word "stroke" is pronounced more like "chooke." "Chooke! Put them down, chooke! Four! Five! Six! . . ." The numbers are bitten off in a tough "street" pronunciation that captures the rhythm of the boat. There are more words of praise for the rowers' efforts: "Yeah, that's the way to be aggressive on it. Okay, goin' after it. Comin' into the last bend. Gonna lace it up loose. Ratings going up to ten. In two. Here we go, on this one, one! Jump on it. Yeah, Let's put this up. Nice job. Block on through."

This power ten has been the peak effort of the practice, but until the boat returns to the dock, Bauer still wants to get more

SETH BAUER (RIGHT), A FRIENDLY presence in anyone's boat, has racked up an impressive record of victories at the World Championships and as an Olympic competitor. Bauer's subtle mix of psychology and humor make him a good model for today's aspiring coxswains.

© Jinsey Dauk

The common crew, with wreaths of poplar boughs

Their temples crown, and shade their sweaty brows:

Besmeared with oil, their naked shoulders shine:

All take their seats, and wait the sounding sign.

They grip their oars; and every panting breast

Is raised by turns with hope, by turns with fear depressed.

The clangor of the trumpet gives the sign;

At once they start, advancing in a line;

With shouts the sailors rend the starry skies;

Lashed with their oars, the smoky billows rise;

Sparkles the briny main, and the vexed ocean fries.

Exact in time, with equal strokes they row:

At once the brushing oars and brazen prow

Dash up the sandy waves, and ope the depths below.

From Book V, The Aeneid,

translated by John Dryden

rowing in this "piece." His commands now are slightly less urgent, but they keep the oarsmen alert: "All the way down, yeah, good five, good squeeze, shift your legs on your seat and your weight on the handle. All the pressure on the handle of the footboard. Yeah, get that quickness." There is one final speedup at the two minute mark: "Let's get set to move up on this one, ratings goin' up, yeah, now the boat's movin', now you send it, reach it along. Get a generation through the stroke. *Send* the boat out. Goin' 30 strokes a minute. Yeah, take a good bite out of it at the front end. Lock into it!"

There is one more power ten up the cox's sleeve and he calls for it with the accustomed praise: "Yeah, that's the way to send it, that's the way to move the boat." Then the power is decreased: "Still in good shape, very nice, let's back off a little more on this one. Yeah. Bring the power down a little more on this one, a little concentration, staying right with it, and we'll bring the power down on this, once more. Lift up. And down, check on starboard."

The eight has arrived back at the dock. To steady the boat, the crew members lift their oars out of the water on command and allow them to wind back down when the cox says so. Their backs are dripping with sweat, and they breathe heavily as their bodies try to recapture the oxygen used during the aerobic workout. The inevitable pain of those successive power tens on this run was not rewarded by a chance at victory. This was only a practice, one of many required to work into racing shape.

For Seth Bauer, it was also a successful workout. He guided the crew, protecting their egos with praise, correcting them in the least punitive way possible. He molded eight large and strong people into a unified entity through the precise timing of his calls and the calm authority of his demands.

During an actual race, the factors a cox must worry about increase many fold. In addition to maintaining form and swing, the crew must deal with its competitors. How the other teams are doing and what to do about it are the cox's main considerations. The skill of a diplomat is required of the cox in competition; strategy is important, articulateness is essential, glibness is favored, and the arts of persuasion are absolutely mandatory.

CHAPTER SIX

A NATIONAL TRADITION

THE OXFORD-CAMBRIDGE BOAT RACE WAS once at the soul of British life in a way that few non-Britishers can understand. Like the relief of Mafeking in the Boer War or Scott's last gasp at the Antarctic, the Boat Race was an eternal reminder of what it means to be British. The Boat Race condensed all the eccentricities and quirky humor of the nation into one annual spree.

The Oxford-Cambridge's oddly poetic qualities may be partly attributable to one of the Boat Race's founders, Charles Wordsworth, nephew of the author of *The Prelude*. As in 1829, when the race was founded, the sheer Britishness of it all can make an outsider gasp. Few foreigners can be expected to appreciate the depth of tradition involved when once a year a nation gathers to see Oxford trounce Cambridge or vice versa.

The Oxford-Cambridge Race has always been a cause for celebration, but in 1881 the oarsmen past and present outdid themselves on a scale that will probably never be equalled. A banquet was scheduled to honor all of the participants in the great race from its founding in 1829 to the year 1881. Representatives of all crews assembled and exchanged speeches. It was found that a majority of

THE OXFORD-CAM-bridge Boat Race evokes nineteenth-century values and raises specters, including some living ones. British novelist Anthony Powell recalled a 1954 Boat Race Party at which the elderly writer, Ivy Compton-Burnett, attended "... wearing a black tricorne for the Boat Race. She was looking formidably severe. I think she was severe. She saw life in the relentless terms of Greek tragedy, its cruelties, ironies—above all its passions—played out against a background of triviality and ennui...." Or maybe she'd just lost a few quid on the Race.

the rowers had become clergymen in the intervening years. Mostly they ate and drank, a Lucullan gorging that brought back memories of the overeating of their college days. They started off with clear mock turtle soup; purée of green peas; and Spring á là Sévigné, as well as salmon in lobster sauce; turbot in Dutch sauce; fillets of sole á là maître d'hôtel; and plain and devilled whitebait. Their appetites whetted, they were then ready for kromeskies á là Russe; sweet-breads á là jardinière; mutton cutlets with mushrooms; roast capons with spaghetti; ham and french beans; boiled fowls; tongues and spinach; saddles and haunches of mutton; and salades á là francaises. The story is that the Chef considered serving the roast capons without spaghetti, but the former oarsmen raised an impossible fuss at the notion.

Then came the second course: guinea fowls, chips, and aspara-gus; jellies; peaches á là Condé; baba cakes au rhum; and iced puddings. The repast was washed down with amontillado sherry, Rhine wine, Rudesheimer 1874, and chablis. There were also champagnes: Pomméry Gréno, Extra Sec 1874, and Sec 1874, as well as liqueurs. The claret was Cos d'Estounel 1875; for port they enjoyed Sandeman's 1842; there was in addition a selection of brown and dry sherries.

To aid prostrate digestive systems, the diners were treated to a program of music, including a "pot-pourri of English National and Nautical Melodies" and selections from *H.M.S. Pinafore* by Gilbert and Sullivan. It was an auspicious celebration of an event with humble beginnings.

In the after-dinner speeches, an old blue recalled his grand-father's rowing exploits at Oxford in 1818, the days when one simply "took off one's coat before exercising and undertook all sorts of exertions in a top hat." One day when the stroke of the Christ Church University boat failed to show up for a race, the captain called out to his granddad, who was standing idly by, "Come step into the boat and row for us." Christ Church won easily. The old man's rowing career did not continue after this triumph. The authorities would not take notice of him because of his round back. After more recollections, the revellers sang Latin odes. The final was translated in part:

Sing we now the glorious dinner
Serv'd in grand Freemason's Hall.
Welcome loser, welcome winner,
Welcome all who've rowed at all;
Oarsmen, steersmen, saint or sinner,
Whet your jaws and to it fall.

Another old-timer remembered the first official Oxford-Cambridge race in 1829. It was only after some years of rowing by themselves

CHANNEL CROSSINGS

*I*F THE BRITISH FIND AMERICANS DIFFICULT TO *collaborate with, imagine how they would find the French. In 1925, a Parisian writer, Pierre MacOrlan, visited the Oxford coach and managed to alienate himself from the Race. MacOrlan bearded the Oxford coach, an "infinitely distinguished young man who gave the impression of not making friends easily." The trainer snapped back at one question from MacOrlan, "Don't ask me anything about who will win the Race. I have no opinion on that. Don't know anything." Peeved, the Frenchman withdrew outside, where he contented himself with making catty comments about the British bobbies observing the Race, their "mouths still wet with beer."*

THE CAMBRIDGE (PREVIOUS PAGE) AND OXFORD (LEFT) crews prepare for the Race. Many mistakenly believe this rowing tradition began in 1829 with the founding of the Race, but it actually goes back at least as far as the year 1035. Around that time, King Canute of England is said to have composed a famous ballad while rowing past the British town of Ely:

> *Merily sang the monkes by Ely*
> *That Canute the King roweth thereby*
> *Roweth, knightes, nearer the lande*
> *And beare we these monke's song.*

Nowadays the Oxford and Cambridge rowers are not likely to hear monks singing as they pass, but other aspects of the annual event are eternal.

that one college decided to challenge the other. For the occasion, the Cambridge boat was directed to "wear their usual white linen shirts with a pink necktie." Even at that early date there was dissent, foreshadowing the perennial stubbornness of rowers: "One man, I well remember, said it was nonsense and would not wear the pink at all." The Oxford crew was marginally more docile about their costume. "Our hats, very sailor-looking, black straws with broad blue ribbons, but not perhaps quite convenient, were, I believe, not long retained," stated another geezer.

In 1836, the Cambridge team changed their colors from pink to light blue quite by accident. They were about to row to the race when it was pointed out that they had no color in the bow. An argument over favorite colors broke out between the members of the

© Peter Spurrier

crew, predictably enough. Finally, an oarsman ran over to a nearby haberdasher's and asked for a piece of Eton blue ribbon. From then on, Cambridge stuck with light blue and Oxford took darker blue.

In 1828, a writer for London's *Sporting Magazine* described the type of rowing physique he considered ideal for the Boat Race: "Not a stumpy, porter-drinking cob, with a short neck, wide shoulders, *et hoc genus omne* of brute strength. My man shall weigh under ten stone; shall be rather loosely than closely put together: let the hinge at the *os coccygis* be well oiled; a fair length of arm, and the heart in the right place." The predilections of this sportswriter suggest that by 1828 rowing was championed by the upper class, the sort of fans who would use a Latin term for the human backside. It was chic to put down the laboring oarsman. Donald Walker, in his book, *Manly Exercises*, published in 1838, derided lower-class rowers in describing a four-man race: "In such a row, a London waterman would have no skin left on his hands; a member of the Funny Boating Club would, we suppose, have no hands left on his arms!"

As rowing grew more popular at Cambridge and Oxford, training methods became serious. Odd practices began to spring up, as well. By the mid-19th century, the Oxford trainer, Archibald MacLaren, published a manual to criticize the dangerous systems then in vogue. On many teams, after the second week of training, if an athlete showed "signs of irritability," he was bled and purged, given a "dose of powerful cathartic. Vomiting may be used when the stomach is foul to get rid of the crudities not cleared by the purging." The rowers were then given a grain of tartar emetic with "ipeca-cuanha, worked off with camomile tea." To complete the training diet, a "blue pill worked off with senna tea" was administered. MacLaren worked himself into a Scots rage at this routine: "How any human body could stand this purging, vomiting, bleeding, with pills anti-bilious and blue, with salts, senna, and camomile, with forced sweating, and restricted liquids and semi-raw flesh, stale bread and few vegetables, is to me incomprehensible." Small wonder, added the trainer, that athletes given this treatment are called "patients" and advisors are told what to do when the rower "falls to pieces."

Despite MacLaren's advice, the harsh training regimens contin-ued. At the turn of the century a widely reprinted guide to rowing advocated giving the oarsman very little to drink to accustom him to thirst, as well as only dry bread-crusts and half cooked meat to build up strength.

Cruelty seemed part of the crew sensibility, and it even extended to animals. W.B. "Guts" Woodgate recalled how the two crews joined the night before a Boat Race to have a "cat hunt." A dog and cat were placed in a room until the "dog got her fangs into puss' windpipe and hung on. It was then only a matter of time." After the "game" was over, the room stank so badly that the athletes had to find other quarters for breakfast. "Guts" dismissed charges of ill treatment of animals with the news that "the cat was under sentence of drowning when we bought her; so she was *mutatis mutandis*, only out of the frying pan into the fire when we gave her a run for life." The animal had its revenge, however; "She actually came back on the morning flood, to reproach us for our cruelty, just as we were launching, We could identify her beyond doubt as she floated by."

Later Boat Race athletes had more refined sensibilities. In 1936, David Haig-Thomas, rowing the same stretch of river with a hangover, was sickened when a "dead dog floated under my oar; of all the things people might do to help, why couldn't they keep the dead dogs away?"

The growing importance of the Boat Race is nowhere clearer than in the many verses written to commemorate the occasion. Contributors include R.C. Lehmann, whose "Trinity Boating Song" supported Cambridge:

> *I met a solid rowing friend, and asked about the Race.*
> *"How fared it with your wind," I said, "When stroke increased the*
> *   pace?*
> *"You swung it forward mightily, you heaved it greatly back.*
> *"Your muscles rose in knotted lumps, I almost heard them crack.*
> *"And while we roared and rattled too, your eyes were fixed like glue.*
> *"What thought went flying through your mind, how fared it,*
> *   Five, with you?"*
> *But Five made answer solemnly, "I heard them fire a gun,*
> *"No other mortal thing I heard until the Race was done."*

The intent of such verses was to infect the lazy reader with the urge to rush to the river and jump in a vessel:

> *They cannot know, who lounge and loaf, the fierce exultant glow*
> *That warms the heart and stirs the pulse when eight men really*
> *   row,*
> *When the banks go wild with roaring, and the roar becomes a*
> *   yell,*
> *And the bowmen feel her dancing as she lifts upon the swell.*
> *And the crowd in chaos blending rend the whelkin with advice—*
> *"Swing out, you've gained, you're gaining, you must get them in*
> *   a trice."*
> *Till with one last stroke we do it, and the coxswain's face grows*
> *   bright,*
> *And it's "Easy all, my bonny boys, you've made your bump to-*
> *   night."*

It would be interesting to see what might happen today if a cox called out, "Easy all, my bonny boys." Another Lehmann ballad entitled "The Oarsman's Farewell to His Oar," features the line, "My hands shall encircle your handle no more," rhyming with "Our last racing stroke has been rowed, oh my oar." R.C. Lehmann has earned the title of Poet Laureate of rowing.

With the assistance of such poet-publicists as Lehmann, crowds for the Boat Race were whipped into feverish excitement. Thomas Hughes, author of the Victorian bestseller *Tom Brown's Schooldays*, described a race in which he ran alongside the river amid a dense crowd, watching Oxford row to victory: "There followed one of the temporary fits of delirium which sometimes seize Englishmen, the sight of which makes one slow to disbelieve any crazy story which is told of the doings of other people in moments of intense excitement. The crew had positively to fight their way into the hotel and barricade themselves there, to escape being carried round Henley on our shoulders." However, the mob was not so easily thwarted: "The enthusiasm, frustrated in this direction, burst out in all sorts of follies, of which you may take this as a specimen: the heavy toll-gate was pulled down and thrown over the bridge into the river by a mob of young Oxonians headed by a small, decorous, shy man in spectacles who had probably never pulled an oar in his life, but who had gone temporarily mad with excitement and I am confident at the moment, would have led his followers not only against the Henley constable, but against a regiment with fixed bayonets." Hughes was grateful that no harm came to the rioters apart from a "few broken heads and black eyes."

Races provided a wild release of pent-up energies during the Victorian era. The humor of crews was expressed in grotesque displays. Guy Nickalls's Oxford crew relaxed training tensions by hiring eight bath chairs, a type of wicker wheelchair for invalids. They were pushed up and down the seaside at Brighton for a lark, and "word was immediately telegraphed to London that all the crew were invalids, and it looked as though the Race would not take place."

The oarsmen were in turn the butt of jokes by aesthetes who looked upon them as muscle-bound barbarians. Max Beerbohm described an Oxford crew pausing in practice to stare at a girl named Zuleika Dobson: "For the moment, these eight young men seemed to have forgotten the awful responsibility that rested on their over-developed shoulders. Their hearts, already strained by rowing, had been transfixed by Eros' darts."

Transatlantic Rivalry

For most of the modern era of Oxford-Cambridge rowing, American oarsmen, often stronger, better trained, and more ambitious than the British, have been imported to participate in the crews. Usually, things have gone fairly smoothly with the international crews. However, twice in the past thirty years, controversies have erupted that caused more publicity than the Boat Race would have otherwise generated.

Transatlantic ventures, with the problem of melding a crew from different training experiences, always bring with them some misunderstandings. An important American rower at Oxford or Cambridge is like a vine transplanted from Napa Valley, California to save the French wine crop. Wine techniques originated in France, as rowing techniques did in England. Two conflicts over dozens of years is not a large price to pay for better rowing. However, both incidents, the first in 1959, the second in 1987, caused enormous uproars.

In 1958, Yale oarsman Reed Rubin arrived at Merton College, Oxford. The British press described the six-foot, four-inch (193-centimeter) Rubin as looking "as if he was hewn by Henry Moore from a piece of Grand Canyon rock." In fact, Rubin was a sophisticated Upper Eastsider from New York who had studied at the Sorbonne. As a Rhodes Scholar, Rubin was given lodgings in a dean's house, but was burdened with menial tasks such as walking the family dog.

During Rubin's first year, Oxford lost the Boat Race. Defeat was new to Rubin and he felt it bitterly. Outspoken and forward,

Courtesy Reed Rubin

Rubin felt he could correct the shortcomings of the Oxford Team. In 1959 he published an article in *Oxford Magazine* in which he spoke his mind on the problems of British rowing. The training system kept the oarsmen on the water far longer than Yale's did, he stated, with notably less success. Moreover, once onshore, the Oxford crew hung around the boathouse, jawing about different theories of sports until Rubin felt stale both mentally and physically. He indicated that some changes were needed, not the least of which was hiring a professional coach. Oxford had always used amateurs.

The recommendations in Rubin's article were ignored by officials of the Boat Club, but a splinter group formed of Oxford blues who followed Rubin. One of the rebel's fathers funded a boat for the eight. Rather than continue with a losing coach, the Englishman "Jumbo" Edwards, Rubin stated that the oarsmen would prefer to be coached over transatlantic phone by his Yale coach.

Words like "pirates" and "mutiny" were bandied about by the press. Yet, the crisis ended not with a bang but a whimper, as another transatlantic American put it. Four of the seceders were prevailed upon to return to the crew; Rubin was not among them. (Nor was another oarsman from Yale who had been ordered by coach Edwards to remove the engineer's hat he had always worn while rowing. The American preferred to quit rather than doff his *chapeau*.) Despite all this brouhaha, Oxford managed to win the Boat Race that year.

They also won in 1987, despite an even more acrimonious debate. Some of the issues were the same, such as the problems of amateur coaching. Yet the manner of dealing with them was different, and this time it was exclusively Americans versus the British.

The successful Oxford coach, Daniel Topolski, knew very well the stretch of river the Race covered. This was particularly important in 1987, when the weather was so foul that victory was a meteorological feat rather than one of rowing skill. On the Oxford crew, a wounded American giant, Chris Clark, had overtrained and wound up with a pulled intercostal muscle before the Race. Coach Topolski judged him not fit to row, and left Clark out of the boat, putting in the Oxford Boat Club President instead. Compounding the American's fury over the decision was their belief that Topolski's unrelenting training program had caused Clark's injury. Topolski's methods were offensive to some of the American rowers because he wanted athletes to spend an unusual amount of time training on both land and water. There were four other Americans on the Oxford crew that year, and they walked out when they heard that Clark would not be in the boat. Rather than offering a compromise that worked within the system, as Reed Rubin tried to do in 1959, the Americans of 1987 said, "love us or lose us." The British decided to choose the latter alternative.

Oxford won the Boat Race, aided by high winds that they had prepared for by using heavy oars and a substance called "speed tape"

Courtesy Reed Rubin

REED RUBIN (FAR LEFT AND ABOVE), FROM NEW YORK'S fashionable Upper East Side, embodied a mythic ideal for British journalists, who described him as "hewn by Henry Moore from a piece of Grand Canyon Rock." Chatting with cox Julian Rowbotham (left) at Merton College, Oxford, Rubin in 1958 was at the height of his athletic intelligence and self-confidence; Oxford traditions didn't stand a chance.

to line the outside of their shell. Yet, the Americans won a moral victory when one of the "rebels," Christopher Penny, was elected Boat Club president for the following year, one of few Americans ever to hold the post. The sometimes uneasy truce between American and British rowers is destined to continue.

Still, amid all these nationalistic squabbles, some Americans and their British counterparts showed that their nations can share some characteristics, notably a taste for vulgar, infantile humor. In a recent year, an American rower gave expert mooning lessons to the "willing pupils amongst the young, fresh-faced, just-out-of-school, Oxford lads," reported coach Dan Topolski. When the whole crew "mounted a full moon," baring their assembled buttocks for the delectation of the Cambridge boatman, that old salt remarked: "They're prettier than their faces, at least."

Apart from mooning, the Oxford rowers lighten the tension of

PRINCIPALS IN THE 1987 BOAT RACE
controversy reveal various aspects of their person-
alities in these photos. Chris Clark (far left, sec-
ond from right) from UCLA rows for Oxford
with the drama of the contest evident on his face.
By contrast, Oxford coach Dan Topolski (left),
shown here after the 1986 defeat of Oxford, is
more emotionally reticent. Meanwhile, Chris
Penny (right), the first American elected presi-
dent of the Oxford crew, was instrumental in es-
tablishing that Topolski's services would no
longer be required for the forthcoming racing
year. Stephen Kiesling's analysis of these goings-
on has appeared in The New Yorker, *along*
with the news that the alleged use of prohibited
speed tape on the Oxford Boat may have helped
to decide the Race.

© Peter Spurrier

the sport by applying offensive nicknames to each other and to the members of opposing teams. One Cambridge crew was known, for example, as The Filth. An athlete in one's own boat might be referred to as Lard, Noddy, Jocker, Worm, Squeaky, Musclemouth, Moron, Woodpecker, Stig, Scrot, Top Pork, Lumpy, Marmite, Half-Wit, Shaky, Angle Dangle, Mean Man, or Bonbons.

The oarsmen will pull the cruellest pranks on one another, with a slap on the back and an "only kidding" to excuse everything afterwards. When Oxford rower Boris Rankov was plagued with several death threats before one year's Race, his teammates were less than sympathetic. They insisted he join them to see the political assassination film, *Day of the Jackal*, before the big day. Rankov was much relieved when his team yelled out "only kidding!"

Beefeater Gin's sponsorship of the Race promised that the atmosphere be lightened up even more. The 1987 Race program included a crew portrait featuring eight large bottles of Beefeater and a tiny one of the coxswain, labelled "a spirited eight." The individual biographies of the crews also reflected a certain "ginny" humor.

Program notes under a photo of the attractive Rowing Secretary Louise Ainsworth ambiguously state that her ambition is to "satisfy the Oxford University Boat Club and all the College Captains at the same time." All the rowers' *vitae* contain attempts at humor, such as one coxswain's life dream to "eat more than he is allowed." On the Cambridge side, Sean B. Gorvy spends his free time "collecting exotic diseases and visiting Addenbrokes Hospital." Another rower in turn "collects exotic diseases from Sean Gorvy." A Cambridge man likes "watching needlework and is fascinated by blowdriers." This is nearly as poetic as the blue who "fancies traveling in silk pajamas." Over the year the Boat Race may have changed, but the enigma of British humor is still intact.

CHAPTER SEVEN

RACING: OTHER REGATTAS

Henley

Henley-on-Thames is the site of the annual race that is perhaps the most quintessential British spectacle, enjoyed almost continuously since its establishment in 1839. Dozens of nations participate in the event. Yet, as Lady Clementine Churchill once told Winston, it is a "lovely pageant of English life." The race was born when the town fathers noted that races were being held on the river at Henley, a perfect natural course. They decided that "from the lively interest which has been manifested at the various boat races," an annual regatta "under judicious and respectable management" would amuse and gratify the neighborhood "from its peculiar attractions." The peculiar qualities of Henley are still intact, not the least of which are the "judicious" Stewards. These zealous protectors, appointed for life, make certain that all conduct is proper for the event. The slightest offense is greeted with a curt, "Not at Henley, please." And that is that.

Gully Nickalls recalled the scene at turn-of-the-century regattas: "Edwardian heyday, blue skies, pink champagne, the razzle-dazzle of the parasol." As a child he was particularly impressed by the lovely ladies present: "Bedecked in swinging, tinkling little jewels, large hats

PLACING A BOAT UPON *the water is as carefully choreographed as any other activity in the sport. As the coxswain calls out a series of numbers and commands, each of the rowers takes care not to let down the side before the proper moment. After all, this is no ordinary practice, but part of the pageantry of the Henley Royal Regatta.*

perched high and lots of pale charmeuse, or pink georgette all gathered at the waist and in cascading flounces falling to the ground." As the women went by, young Nickalls could hear a distant military band playing the "Merry Widow Waltz," suddenly changing to "Pale Hands I Loved Beside the Shalimar," with an impressive cornet solo.

This spectacle of Edwardian calm also features some disturbances that are gleefully anticipated by the spectators. For instance, one year Gully Nickalls sank in a pairs boat at Henley. Decades later, people still asked him eagerly about the time his boat capsized, "amidst execrations that were visible but inaudible at the winning post." Nickalls was a bit miffed that the crowd "would rather see people swimming by accident than rowing in earnest."

There are very few things that can truly upset Henley. World War II did, but not permanently. The official history of Henley, in two volumes, includes a dry observation for the year 1945: "The war in Europe having ended in May, it was decided to hold a one-day Regatta on Saturday, July 7th."

More lasting upsets have been caused by the introduction of foreign visitors. Russians, who first appeared in 1954, caused much acrimony. A British rowing historian noted that "true to form, the Russians began by complaining." When they won the Grand Challenge Cup, they wanted to "form up behind an enormous red banner bearing the hammer and sickle, whilst the band played *their* national anthem." The Stewards shook their fingers and said, "Not at Henley, please." The Russians were not through. The Soviet pairs team received illicit signals from their coach who was seated in the umpire's launch. Contrary to the rules, the coach was steering his rowers away from obstacles. Gully Nickalls, then a Henley official,

arranged for another passenger in the umpire's launch to strike the Soviet coach a "violent blow on the arm." The Russian got the message, especially after Nickalls cornered him and spoke loudly and slowly, "YOU MUST LEARN NOT TO CHEAT AT GAMES." Perhaps to make amends, a Russian official presented Nickalls with a copy of a book he had written in Russian on oarsmanship. The volume turned out to be a complete plagiarism, down to the illustrations, of a book Nickalls himself wrote some decades before.

Meanwhile, for the British rowers, victory at Henley has always justified any sort of manners. Henley was usually considered to be more important than academics. In 1931, three Cambridge students left their training sessions briefly in order to pick up their degrees in person, as required. The coach, Sir Henry Howard, was livid at this breach of training discipline: "Degrees! Bugger degrees! If

THE CROWDS AT HENLEY ARE POLITELY ENTHRALLED BY the spectacle. Either they lounge in neat rows of director's chairs, wondering if they should have another helping of cold lobster and strawberry tea, or if they should stand at respectful distances from one another, watching the rowers pass. There is none of the rude pushing and shoving you might see at less authentically British sports events.

© Patrick Ward/Wheeler Pictures

I knew there were chaps up to this sort of business, they wouldn't have been in the Henley crew!"

At Cambridge's Lady Margaret Boat Club in 1934, some rowdy athletes lessened their tensions as Henley approached by pouring "quantities of beer and other things" on a passing proctor. The Dean was sent for and was announced by the Head Porter: "Gentlemen, the Dean." The oarsmen replied, "Fuck the Dean!" "Thank you, gentlemen," replied the Dean. Then he asked, "Would you kindly make less noise. Good night, gentlemen." And the Dean left. From that day forward, whenever the Dean was mentioned in the Boat Club, it was always with the ritual incantation, "The Dean, fuck-the-dean . . ."

According to another Lady Margaret Boat Club story, one captain coached so vigorously for Henley, that he "spat his false teeth . . . into the river." In a preliminary race for the same regatta, rowers had the joy of hearing an oarsman named Tito Arias, son of the president of Panama, announced over the public address system as "Mr. Hairy-Arse, winner of the Maiden Sculls."

The real thrill of Henley, though, is the aura of tradition. Earthly glory is transitory, but there is always Henley.

Harvard and Yale

First held in 1852 on Lake Winnipesaukee in New Hampshire, the American version of the Oxford-Cambridge Boat Race took place in

THE PARTIAL CROWD THEIR HOPES
and fears divide,
And aid with eager shouts, the favored side.
Cries, murmurs, clamors, with a mixing sound,
From woods to woods, from hills to hills
rebound. . . .
Now board to board the rival vessels row;
The billows lave the skies, and ocean groans
below.

From Book V, The Aeneid,
translated by John Dryden

YALE VARSITY IN 1914 (ABOVE); HAR-vard J.V. in 1941 (left), both in the classic crew team pose. Note the seriousness of expression on the faces of the Harvard team. Obviously, among other things, this photo was meant to intimidate future opponents. The Yale team seems a bit more vulnerable, with their more relaxed stances and casual attire. Then one notices the lucky horseshoe above the boathouse door and wonders if they feel it helps them through competitions.

many locations before the course was settled in New London, Connecticut in 1878. The Harvard-Yale race can never have the national importance that its British counterpart, Cambridge-Oxford, has had. However, as rowing becomes more popular in America, the Harvard-Yale race is a natural focus for spectators' attention.

A century ago, rowing enthusiasts in the United States took rowing more to heart. Perhaps because travel by water in a ferry or rowboat was more common, crowds did not see the racing eight as an anachronism. In the April, 1893 issue of *Century Magazine*, a story was published about an athlete's feelings as he rowed in the Harvard-Yale match. The Yalie "envies the phlegmatic, countrybred fellow rowing at bow, who afterwards avowed that he thought nothing at all, and who is the best conditioned of the lot." The Yalie observes the flotilla of yachts nearby and gives a thought to "Trix," his sweetheart. Meanwhile, the Harvard eight are busy "stripping the jerseys from great muscles and mighty beef." Jack's feeling of comparative inferiority is lessened when he looks ahead of him at his teammates' "line of sun-burned shoulders and lean, lithe bodies." As the crowd chants the chorus from Aristophanes' *The Frogs* as a Yale war cry, "Brek-kek-kek-kek-ko-ax-ko-ax," they win.

In essence, the feelings described by the author of 1893 are not different from those of Steve Kiesling and later scribes of the Harvard-Yale Race. But how far we have strayed from those days may be seen in the program of the Harvard-Yale Race of 1895. A book-sized affair, the program cost 25 cents, and included advertisements for miniature Harvard-Yale souvenir pocket watches. There were photos of all the college teams of both schools, not just rowing, but baseball and football too. Even the drama clubs were depicted. The Yale Dramatic Organization photo features two rows of lovely young ladies dressed in turn-of-the-century garb, perfect Gibson girls. On close inspection, these women turn out to be male undergraduates in extremely convincing drag, circa 1895. Transvestism and rowing were considered good, clean college fun. Then, rowing represented college youth as much as any activity.

© Paul Thompson/FPG Intl.

THIS PAIR OF PHOTOS IS OBVIOUSLY another attempt by Yale (left) and Harvard (right) to intimidate each other before they actually meet on the river. Undoubtedly, there are twin photos for every year of the great rivalry between these schools.

Robert Visser

THE CANTABRIGIANS OF MASSACHUSETTS ARE USUALLY drawn to the water, but on the day of the Head of the Charles Regatta (left and following pages), they crowd the piers and bridges. They peer at the rowers going by and reflect upon the not too distant time when the Charles River provided the lifeline for the residents of the town, and rowing was a necessity, not just a sport. Those days are gone, but the party-colored banners and garb speak of festive individualism, a Massachusetts tradition since the founding of the Republic.

The Head of the Charles

The regatta called the Head of the Charles is another take-off on a British event, the Head of the River, which Steve Fairbairn founded in 1926. For those who see the Olympics as commercialized and politicized, the Head of the Charles is an event still run by the athletes. Boycotts never occur at the Head of the Charles; terrorists have never murdered anyone. Instead, crowds are drawn to the celebratory display of flags flying, multicolored jerseys and other paraphernalia. The pageantry is so bright and optimistic that older rowers who are encouraged to participate scarcely stop to think about their diminishing strength. As one participant cheerfully noted, "We're just a bunch of old farts going out to have some fun."

Some of the master rowers wear T-shirts with the slogan, THE OLDER WE GET, THE BETTER WE WERE. One middle-aged man offered an explanation as to why the Head of the Charles and other regattas appeal to men of his era: "It's terrific to have a support system of experienced, middle-aged men. There's a rediscovery of one's sense of maleness. It's something you can lose sense of in a marriage, where everything is being compromised and negotiated. It's a thrill to find that men are really different from women and have their own way of pulling together. It's a way of making a positive thing out of your mid-life crisis."

So, every year, amid the youthful fun-seekers at the Head of the Charles, the sort who are photographed for the fashion tabloids, plenty of older folk are also present.

REGATTA

106

The Nile Regatta

One of the most unexpected results of Henry Kissinger's Middle Eastern diplomacy in the mid-1970s was an invitation to Americans to compete in the Nile Regatta. Some people grumbled cynically that the only reason Kissinger worked so hard for peace in the Middle East was to give his alma mater, Harvard, a chance to win on the Nile. Whatever Kissinger's motivation, due to his successful cultivation of Egyptian relations, the Harvard and Yale teams flew over to Egypt in 1974.

The one-time-only Nile Regatta was meant as a reenactment of competitions dating back to 1400 B.C., in which the winning team was given the honor of leading the funerary processions of a dead pharaoh across the Nile. It is unknown whether these ancient Egyptian crews were then buried along with the dead king, a fate suffered by favorite servants and pets. The crews paraded to the accompaniment of the Triumphal March from Verdi's *Aida*, while Egyptian schoolchildren threw rose petals in their paths. At first, the competition went as expected. Harvard won the first race, held in Luxor (ancient Thebes) in front of the temple of Ramses II. However, before the second leg of the race, held in Cairo, Harvard stroke Al Shealy, came down with bronchitis. Although Shealy was known in the rowing community for his imitations of George C. Scott in the role of General Patton, not one to abandon ship easily, he had to withdraw. With the Harvard Crew rowing at less than their best, the Cairo Police Rowing Club triumphed, as much to their own surprise as to everyone else's.

The Olympics

For those who can accept the commercialism, the politics, and all the other distractions, the Olympics can be a mightily exciting endeavor. No matter if rowing is a non-visual sport, certain images from the 1984 Olympics at Lake Casitas have lasting impact. There is the amazing feat of Perrti Karppinen. The single sculler kept his boat hovering steadily like a barracuda, then charged ahead of Peter-Michael Kolbe in the last five hundred meters. There is also the triumph of Americans Brad Lewis and Paul Enquist who captured the gold in the doubles race, a phenomenal feat on many accounts. They started out dead last, then relentlessly rowed through the competition. After the race, Lewis, grinning in victory and unshaven, resembled a sly demon perched on the back of St. Anthony in a Renaissance painting. The tonsured Enquist filled in for the Saint.

The United States men's rowing eight placed behind the surprise victors from Canada at the same Games. During the awards

© Robert Visser

THIS IS THE SORT OF OVER-THE-shoulder glance Brad Lewis (left) might give an opponent before pulling ahead to gut out another victory. His unshaven look is quite deliberate, intended to convince his opponent of the seriousness of the task at hand, and perhaps to unsettle him a bit too—just in case tonsorial variations have any effect at the dire stages of a race.

AT THE 1984 OLYMPICS IN LAKE
Casitas, the Canadian quads (below) made an
impressive showing. Perhaps most remarkable,
though, was the Canadian eight, which suprised
everyone, possibly including the crew members
themselves, by walking away with the gold.

*AT THE CRUCIAL MOMENT OF THE START, THE CREWS ARE
already in motion. It is well known that the first crew to start without being
caught will have an excellent chance to win the race. So, when the starter actually says "Partez," serious competitors will have already begun.*

© Dominik Keller

*IN THE 1984 OLYMPICS, JOHN BIGLOW (FOLLOWING PAGE)
did his damnedest, and it just was not enough to win a medal. He had made
the team in 1980, but America's withdrawal for political reasons prevented
his competing. Then, he made the team again in 1984 despite a herniated
disk. To watch the videotape of Biglow racing through the final few moments of the sculling event, knowing that he will place fourth, is a most dis-
tressing experience.*

ceremony some Americans looked deeply saddened, as if they had blown the race by receiving the silver medal. Strikingly handsome Edward Ives managed a smile for the TV cameras. His teammate Andy Sudduth could not even fake a convincing grin.

The American women's eight proudly received their gold medals on the awards platform, sisterhood personified. The Rumanian women's silver medal eight offered their own bit of drama when one oarswoman fainted as she was presented with her medal.

If one is familiar with the rowers' histories and personalities, one can root for them at the Olympics as ardently as for athletes in any sport. The battle continues between Sudduth, Karppinen, Kolbe, and Lange, but other boats offer a festive exhibition as well. When the Italian pair-with-cox won the gold in 1984, the coxswain ecstatically splashed the water around him like a toddler in a playpool. At the World Championships, the same cox evoked another emotive tribute after a first place finish. The rower farthest from him climbed over his partner in the boat to embrace the little cox *all'Italia*.

By contrast the start of each race is a moment of tangible tension. The rowers are poised, still, ready. The counter calls off the boats, in French, asking each in turn, *"Êtes-vous prêts?"* ("Are you ready?"). French, the international rowing language, captures the arch coldness of the moment, the ordeal until the race begins. The moment may stretch into an eternity as one boat after another has a "false start," a crew's way of saying that they are not ready. Finally the counter chants a highly rhythmic, *"Êtes-vous prêts?"* Days before the race, coxswains take their crews down to the water to hear individual starters' quirks of pronunciation. A fast start cannot be missed because the rowers couldn't understand the counter. The final *"Êtes-vous prêts?"* is like a baseball pitcher's windup, then the *"partez"* is spit out like a fastball.

Every crew must start at the syllable *"par-"* or be lost in the other boats' wakes. Coaches advise the rowers not to even wait to hear the sound *"par-"* or consciously register it, but to be gone when it *should* be there. The result is that many starts seem to jump the gun, but that is far better than losing an inch in an Olympic race.

In the instant between *"Êtes-vous prêts?"* and *"partez,"* many long-retired oarspeople listen anxiously, as if they themselves were on the water at that moment. The instinctive response to *"partez"* is, in a veteran rower, unconscious—when you hear *"partez,"* you go.

After the *"partez"* the electrified anxiety of the start bursts out. The amplified metallic voices of the coxswains shriek a dozen different languages. Fortunate is the rower who can block out every voice but his or her own coxswain's. Some coxes talk continually to drown out the distracting voices of the competition. Who can forget the nightmarish sight of the 1984 Rumanian pair-with-cox? The cox appeared as but a tiny head emerging from the bottom of the boat, talking incessantly. What could he have been saying all that time? No

American rower would have tolerated that talking head. With a well-placed kick, overboard he would have gone to talk to the fish in Lake Casitas.

There were no rowing events at the first modern Olympics in 1896 because the weather was inauspicious. Four years later, however, the great tradition began and British superiority, especially in sculling, was established early on. In 1908, a 40-year-old Englishman, Harry Blackstaffe, defeated an opponent half his age. In 1924 in Paris, the great Jack Beresford defeated American William Garrett Gilmore. Gilmore later recalled he was distracted during the race: "During the last 200 meters, when it seemed to get hotter with every stroke and I was making the supreme effort to grasp victory, a kindly breeze swept across the Seine, carrying a strong but pleasant scent from a perfumery which was not within sight. It was truly so strong that it first gagged me, but in a moment I was rowing on as if in a flowing river of the perfume." Brought down by the minions of Chanel, Gilmore lost by two-and-a-half lengths.

Four years later, Australian sculler Henry Pearce also faced distraction, but this one did not get the better of him. In the middle of the race, a single file of ducks passed in front of his boat. Pearce paused to let them pass, then sped on to a victory of five lengths. One shudders to think what some of today's more gung-ho athletes might have done in this situation.

The odd poultry theme in sculling was revived in 1956 when a professional chicken-sexer, the Australian Stuart Mackenzie, lost in the final to Soviet star Vyacheslav Ivanov. The Russian, only eighteen years old, was so exultant that he threw his gold medal into the air. It fell somewhere in Melbourne's Lake Wendouree. Ivanov immediately leapt in after his award, but he could not recover it. The Olympic committee generously gave him a replacement. Ivanov also won the sculling gold in 1960 and 1964, setting a three-time record.

Ivanov rowed so hard for his final victory in 1964 that he blacked out before the finish. He recalled in his memoir, *Winds of Olympic Lakes*, "I don't remember how long it was before I gradually came to . . . I gathered the last bits of my strength, lifted my head, and could not believe it. Clear water was ahead of me and no one in front, with fifty meters to finish. I wondered if I was delirious, seeing things. . . ." Ivanov picked himself up from the bottom of his boat and rowed to victory.

If sculling is the archetypal Olympic challenge, the pairs race offers its own interesting drama in the combination of two personalities in a single boat. In 1948, the pairs-without-cox race was won by two Englishmen, John Wilson and William Laurie. They had placed first at Henley ten years before, but had not had a chance to row since then, because of World War II. In 1948, they picked up their oars again, and after six weeks of training they triumphed at Henley. After a few more months of practice, they swept to the Olympic gold. As they had both been in military service in the Sudan, this pair was known fondly as the "Desert Rats."

An even unlikelier pair of victors emerged in 1952 in Helsinki. Americans Charles Logg and Thomas Price of Rutgers University had never rowed pairs at all until eight weeks before the Olympics. Price, age 19, had only begun to row six months before. Those were ideal days for collegiate athletes with Olympic aspirations. Nowadays the level of training is so high that few college rowers have any chance to make the Olympic team.

East Germany offered its own unknown pairs team as well. A popular radio comic, Heinz Quermann, played a role in their recruitment. In 1969, he announced in his routine that tall kids should sign up for rowing with the Leipzig Sports Club. Two sixteen-year-olds, Wolfgang Mayer and Siegfried Brietzke, responded. This pair won the gold in Munich in 1972, and became known as "der Quermannpaar," after the funnyman who united them.

Families have always worked well together in boats. Perhaps the most extended family alliance occurred in 1936, when the victorious four-with-cox from France, bronze medallists, included Fernand Vandernotte, his brother Marcel, and his twelve-year-old son as cox.

In larger boats, where the cox has more strategic importance, older and wiser minds usually prevail. In the 1964 Olympics in Tokyo, America's gold medal eight from the Vesper Club was coxed by 46-year-old Robert Zimonyi, a Hungarian-American accountant. Zimonyi coxed for the Hungarian Olympic teams in 1948 and 1956. His participation as an American made him one of the oldest gold medallists in Olympic rowing history.

Drama, thrills, fear, anxiety: the Olympics has all this, and ludicrousness, too. New training strategies can be revealed, as the 1932 Japanese crew with a new stroke technique. They rowed along at twenty-eight strokes per minute, then at an instant's notice raised their rating to forty-four, or even fifty strokes per minute. One bemused American rower compared the noise they made to a "flock of ducks taking off." The Japanese crew was not notably successful with this new form of rowing, but a legend was born: somehow it was rumored that a Japanese crew managed to sustain the 50-stroke rate for an entire race and then collectively met their maker at the finish line. This farfetched anecdote has been halfway accepted even by such models of probity as Steve Kiesling in his book, *The Shell Game*. Apart from its banzai attractiveness as a yarn, however, it has no basis in fact.

The Olympics seem to exist for the propagation of such stories. The auspicious games are the natural breeding grounds for the creation of athletic mythology, especially when imaginative oarspeople encounter eccentric new techniques every four years.

CHAPTER EIGHT

BOATHOUSES AND ROWING COURSES

B Y THE MYSTERIES OF ARCHITECTURE, THE boathouse has come to be much more than a house for boats. Built by boat clubs with a sense of permanence and pride, as representative of different eras of design, boathouses have won many advocates over the years, including some surprising ones. The poet Marianne Moore was well known as a baseball fan. In 1965, at the age of 78, she paused in rooting for her favorite team long enough to write a letter to the Park Slope Civic Council, "imploring" the director to "allow our boathouse in Prospect Park to remain. We in Brooklyn admire it. No substitute would appease us." The Prospect Park gem was saved.

A string of beautiful, if run down, boathouses can be found at "Boathouse Row" in Philadelphia, one of the Schuylkill River's most venerable institutions. The houses date back to the organization of the Schuylkill Navy in 1858, the oldest amateur athletic board in America. At the time, the boathouses were small frame structures in Fairmount Park, nestled at the foot of "Lemon Hill." Then as now, urban violence was a problem. Parts of the Park were unprotected by police, so neighborhood "toughs" frequently robbed the houses. Before too long, the city granted permission to build larger and

BOATHOUSE ROW IN *Philadelphia is a unique area that deserves the status of National Historic Monument. The houses themselves, of which Vesper is visible in the background here, are dilapidated through loving overuse. Repairs might be made someday, but the boathouses are in such constant use that there never seems to be a good time to interrupt the daily activity. Nevertheless, the beautiful buildings remain an inspiration to any rower.*

RESOLVED THAT ANY MEMBER MARRYING shall forfeit a dozen of champagne to the club which shall be drunk by the members of the club at such time and place as shall be agreed upon by them.

Resolution made by Pembroke Club in Dublin, 1840.

"more pretentious" houses as a way of protecting the equipment within. However, it was ruled that the new buildings must be "architecturally neat and attractive" in order to "enhance the picturesqueness of the River bank." Stone and brick were to be used as building materials.

The Undine Barge Club of Philadelphia is a typical example of boathouse development. The organization was formed in 1856 with the object of "healthful exercise, relaxation from business, friendly intercourse, and pleasure." The oarsmen bought a barge and built a shed to store it in, fifty feet (fifteen meters) long by eight feet (two-and-a-half meters) wide. The shed cost one hundred dollars. Owning a building gave the club a need to identify itself. However, naming the Club was not as easy a task as building the shed. Among the

rejected names were Irene, Wyoming, Beauty, Nymph, Juno, Albert, Leni-Lenape, Arab, Gazelle, and Jewess. Finally, Undine was chosen after the eponymous heroine of the sentimental tale by De la Motte Fouqué about an underwater nymph of the "babbling brooks." There is something comic about a bunch of burly rowers naming the club after a fey novella.

After establishment of the club, meetings were scheduled, and absent members were fined twenty-five cents and latecomers ten cents. Other fines were levied upon the members to help pay for the new edifice. Coxswains faced the most stringent regulations. Running a boat aground cost a cox fifty cents, while "tyrannical or ungentlemanly conduct" cost five dollars, a solid sum in those days. Among the other proscribed practices was criticizing the cook.

THE BUILDINGS ON BOATHOUSE ROW
are all distinguished, but they offer one master-
piece, the Undine Barge Club (left, center), de-
signed by the great architect Frank Furness.

THE NEWELL BOATHOUSE ON THE CHARLES RIVER
is the setting of fond memories of many Harvard alumni. Most, it is certain, agree with the sentiments Kenneth Grahame expressed in **The Wind in the Willows:** *"There is nothing—absolutely nothing—half so much worth doing as simply messing about in boats . . . or with boats . . . In or out of 'em, it doesn't matter."*

No sooner had the boathouse been paid for than troubles began. In 1857 the club was the target of burglars who stole everything but the boat and oars. The boathouse was stripped clean again in 1858. For gatherings, the members retreated to a hotel and the city eventually condemned the original building. Finally, in 1882 the established members chipped in fourteen thousand dollars for a two-story boathouse of undressed brown stone, with a conical roof tower on its east side. The architect was the great Philadelphian, Frank Furness. The first floor, with thirteen-foot (four-meter) high ceilings, contained the boat storage room. The upper floor had a dressing room thirty by fifty feet (nine by fifteen meters), with colored cathedral glass windows and roof windows overhead. A large Nuremberg window with a fine view was also included. Next to the dressing room were the Ladies' Reception Room and the Members' Room. In the latter, a tiled fireplace bore painted scenes from the legend of Undine. Over the mantle was an engraving of Frederick De La Motte Fouqué. Banners, plaques, and photographs decorated the Ladies' Room; among the celebrities represented were the great team rowers, the Ward Brothers. All interior walls were in native hardwood, oiled or varnished. It is a shame that today the Undine and other clubs of Boathouse Row are so dilapidated, though still used and loved by rowers.

Although it was claimed that "no attempt has been made at elaborate decoration or ornamentation," many nineteenth-century boathouses were in fact proud examples of cultural elegance. Perhaps the artistic urge to versify about rowing, largely absent today, can be compared to this early desire to legitimize a sport with lovely architecture. Beautiful boathouses continued to be built into the early years of the twentieth century. As architectural styles changed, however, some of the wind seemed to leave the sails of the boathouse builders. The smooth, white, super-clean surfaces of the International Style of the early century, though plainly energetic and sportive, might have suited any sport and did not seem to embody the stylized grandeur of crew. The new boathouses in this style lacked something of the sense of protection and warmth evoked by the solid structures of the past. Like an antique carousel or other pleasure edifices, an old boathouse has come to symbolize a more gracious era gone by.

© M. L. Thomas

ACROSS THE RIVER FROM NEWELL IS THE BEAUTIFUL WELD
Boathouse. Built in 1905, this gracious dwelling is today home to the Rad-cliffe Crew and the Boston Rowing Center.

THESE HARLEM RIVER REGATTA
*trophies date from various years and symbolize
the traditions and pageantry that continue to
make rowing such a unique sport.*

The Harlem River Speedway

The tradition of rowing along the Harlem River Speedway course in New York City dates back to before the founding, in 1866, of the Harlem Regatta Association. Mile-long races were rowed from below the George Washington Bridge to Fordham Heights. In the afternoon, races were rowed in the reverse direction. By 1905, what had come to be called "Sculler's Row" included the clubs Nassau, Harlem Metropolitan, Wyanoke, Crescent, and the First Bohemian Boat Club. The latter was a particularly influential organization, as the members, mostly from Czechoslovakia, were very avid oarsmen. At the turn of the century, a Bohemian Boat Club member was President of the entire Harlem Regatta. His name was F. Kafka, although it is certain he was not the famous writer, who nevertheless was fond of rowing.

An appealing feature of this uptown course was its popularity with high school crews. The Bohemian Juniors and the Dewitt Clinton High School teams excelled in the beginning of this century. Called "the Schoolboy Oarsmen," they would battle it out in intense rivalries. Their classmates would follow the races, running along the speedway and "creating a miniature stampede," according to one newspaper account. Even in 1907, a main feature of these races was maneuvering the boat around the debris floating in the water.

One of the most ardent boathouse-preservation battles took place in 1936, between the Waverly Boat Club and the New York City Parks Commissioner Robert Moses. The Waverly Club, one of the oldest in America, was found in 1859. Its boathouse rested on piles built into the Hudson River at 167th Street, along Sculler's Row. The house itself, a lavish three-story edifice, was purchased in 1907 from the Passaic Rowing Club, and transported in pieces from New Jersey. It was filled with shells and trophies, mementoes of almost a century of rowing. None of this interested Robert Moses, the "power broker," for the Waverly Boathouse stood right in the path of what he intended to be Riverside Drive.

Times were bad for the Club. In the depths of the Depression, membership had dwindled to thirty. They knew that if forced to go, they could not afford to build another boathouse; they couldn't even afford to move the one they were using. Moses offered no consolation. He ordered the club to vacate "on or before September tenth," but the message was only received on September tenth. The club members feared that they had no choice but to quietly disband. Then a temporary solution was found when a construction company donated a barge to the club. The Waverly Boat Club built a small replica of their former home, then floated it on a portion of the River not coveted by Robert Moses. There is a kind of poetic justice in the Club finding refuge on the waters.

Last-minute heroics by the Club President dramatized the incident even more. When five racing shells floated loose during the moving process, the president, T. Ormond Deignan, dove into the waters to save them. However, this passionate display of devotion did not sway the Parks Commissioner from his course. The demolition of the Waverly Boathouse took longer than Moses expected; buildings were soundly built in those days. Still, by the end of November, the boathouse had been levelled.

In its place, Moses built the 79th Street boat basin, which serves the many indiscriminately, as opposed to the few dozen privileged who made use of the Waverly Club. This incident occurred in 1936, when Franklin Roosevelt was proclaiming the era of the common man. In this vein, Moses chalked up a victory for mass consumption, but destroyed a distinguished building.

The Club Life

The Leander Club has long been one of Britain's most august rowing institutions, and its place in history is secure, if somewhat imprecise. Reportedly founded in 1818, the Club adopted the hippopotamus as its official insignia, because it "was the only aquatic animal apart from the members of *Leander*, which kept its nose permanently above in the air." The elitism of the group did not lessen their competitive spirit. On the contrary, the sensitive members often suffered for their sporting efforts. After one race in 1831, "the exertions at the conclusion of the contest became lamentably apparent. Captain Shaw nearly fainted and had to be carried ashore. Mr. Bayford was obliged to retire to bed, as was one of the Oxford gentlemen. The others were more or less exhausted." Despite these casualties, the victors were greeted by cheers, cannons, and a "*feu-de-joie* was fired."

In the early 1830s the Leander rowers wore white hats, green silk neckerchiefs, and white trousers. As one contemporary put it, their appearance "gave additional gaiety to the scene." In 1852 the Leander boat sank in mid-race. An oarsman called out to the Leander stroke, "Give me your oar, sir, to hang on by, for I cannot swim." The stroke "gallantly tossed him the oar, saying, 'Nor can I.'"

In those days oarsmen felt they must behave like ancient heroes. After fouling out of the Henley Regatta in 1841, the Leander Club reacted in Achillean fashion: "They retired to their tents to nurse their wrath." From these heroic beginnings, Leander has managed to maintain itself over the years.

In contrast to Leander's gentlemanly conduct, the San Diego Rowing Club was egalitarian from its founding in 1881. The S.D.R.C. excluded no one, as it had the mandate of being a "truly plain club, minus frills." Frills were certainly absent from early photos of semi-nude sunbathers at the Club, who referred to themselves fondly as "gabooners."

This casual attitude may have caused problems in fundraising, especially when women were allowed to participate. In *The Rowing Club Man*, the San Diego group's newsletter, the following women's

Courtesy Reed Rubin

fund-raising appeal was published in 1918: "Oftentimes, Miss or Missus SDRC admiree will say to herself, why can't we, too, have an all-joy place like the Rowing Club, to bask in the sunshine and splash in the refreshing waters of the Bay? . . . Here's a real chance for some good-hearted well-to-do to establish just such a club and thereby build an everlasting memorial to himself."

Despite such good-natured appeals, the women did not receive their "all-joy place," a separate building for themselves. Funds were low and the women were gradually eased out of the organization entirely. In 1922 the San Diego Club minutes announced that "ladies changing their clothes at the clubhouse was agreed undesirable and strictly forbidden." Not until 1974 was a woman again admitted to the San Diego Club. Until then, Club events had the all-male air of

fraternity hijinks in the early films of Laurel and Hardy. A program survives from a SDRC Luau in 1938 with the translation "native feast" as the subtitle. Costumes were prescribed for the event: "Ladies to wear slacks or grass skirts, Men in Whites or Go Native." Included on the program were "Dancing - Eats - Hawaiian Entertainment," along with the dire words of warning, "Positively no Stags." After the Second World War, the Club suffered a decline and the old boathouse was preserved only as a restaurant.

As always, even among recreational rowers, stubbornness resulted in arguments. A stellar member of the SDRC in the 1940s and the 1950s, Earl Kyle took the somewhat perverse view that swimming was far more important an activity to the Club than rowing was. So adamant was Kyle in his orations about the benefits

Courtesy Reed Rubin

swimming offered that his name duly appears in the Club historical records as Earl "Esther Williams" Kyle.

Such joshing was meant as part of the overall friendliness of the SDRC. Peppy slang is featured in *The Rowing Club Man* newsletter of May 1918, urging members to use the official club greeting: "Hello, Charley! . . . Rowing Club folk have always been noted for their wonderful hospitality . . . It's up to each man to assist in fostering the grand ol' spirit and give the Hello, Charley! with a ring to fellow clubsters at all hours . . . So let's give the ol' smile, folks, and keep the famous greeting a-going full force. It pays."

SDRC President Alonzo D. Jessop said essentially the same thing when he noted in 1913, "A man doesn't realize what life means until he has tasted a little of our club life."

AMERICAN, REED RUBIN (ABOVE, SEATED UNDER THE parasol; left, seated front in the dark suit, without a hat) and his teammates of the Merton College, Oxford Boat Club, are up to bighish jinks. Obviously, the rower's life is more than just rigorous training and give-it-your-all competitons. Notice that in both photos, Rubin is looking away from the camera, perhaps an indication of his "mutinous" spirit.

CHAPTER NINE

EQUIPMENT

N EVER CROSS A BOATMAN!

In 1961 the Columbia University crew was foolhardy enough to fire their boatwright on short notice one Saturday morning. Within the hour, there were huge gaping holes in eight of the crew's best racing shells. The boatwright was arrested on a charge of "malicious mischief," but $80,000 worth of damage had already been done, and the Columbia crew had learned a valuable lesson.

To have their shells repaired, there was only one place for the Columbia crew to go: Seattle, Washington, the home of the great Pocock boat empire. The Pocock family has reigned supreme in the field of rowing equipment since the end of the nineteenth century in England, when a boat-builder named Pocock furnished boats for the African explorer Henry Stanley ("Dr. Livingstone, I presume"). Boats for jungle jaunts did not satisfy Pocock's soul, so he began designing racing shells. His son Frederick Pocock carried on the family business, building shells for Eton, Oxford, and Cambridge. Another son, William, became a world sculling champion and coach at Westminster School. Frederick Pocock's son George won races in a twenty-six-pound (twelve-kilogram) pine shell he had built himself

HE KEEPS HIS STURDY legs applied
Just where he has been taught to,
And always moves his happy slide
Precisely as he ought to.

From "The Perfect Oar," R.C. Lehmann

© Robert Visser

127

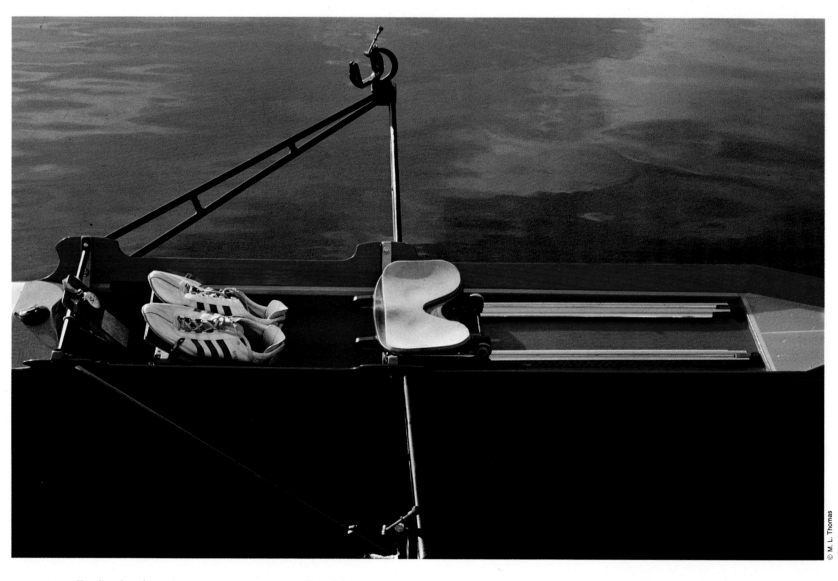

at age 17. Fred's daughter Lucy was women's sculling champ of England in 1910–11.

In 1912, George Pocock and his brother William emigrated to Vancouver, British Columbia, perhaps to escape the ties of family tradition. The first thing they did was set up a boatbuilding concern. They soon moved to Seattle, where they had headquarters on campus at the University of Washington until 1926, when they moved once again, to the north end of Lake Union. There they established such a successful business that almost anyone who rowed in the first three-quarters of this century has used a Pocock shell.

George Pocock, with his son Stan, who carried on the business after his father's retirement, was a craftsman of the old school; what Amati and Guarneri were to violins and cellos, the Pococks were to racing shells. They spared no effort to building the very best, and the

results can be seen in shells still admired for their look, feel, and effectiveness.

Over many decades, George Pocock tried almost every conceivable type of wood and method of construction. His experiments resulted in dramatic improvements in sculls. By the mid-1920s, Pocock's designs were so superior to the competition that his boats monopolized college regattas. Pocock provided the United States Navy with the boats used by the Naval Academy in their thirty-one year winning streak. United States Olympic crews for generations went for the gold in Pocock shells. In sum, at one point about eighty percent of American college sculls were made by George's company.

Among Pocock's innovations were lightweight oars, a new type of oarlock, sliding seats, and a device for steering that combined a fin and a rudder. This apparatus was placed under the cox's seat instead

STANDARD EQUIPMENT TODAY, THE sliding seat (right) was introduced in the 1870s and improved upon by the boat-building Pocock family, who has been the leader in rowing equipment since the end of the nineteenth century. By the 1920s, the Pocock company had become so dominant, in fact, that the family made eighty percent of all sculls for American colleges.

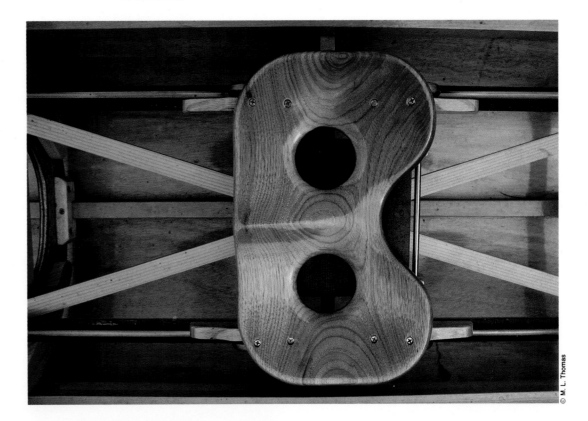

© M. L. Thomas

© M. L. Thomas

WOODEN SHELLS (LEFT) HAVE LAGGED in popularity since the introduction of fiberglass models, which have proved to be faster, cheaper, and easier to maintain. Yet the handcrafted version is unparalleled in beauty and will always appeal to recreational rowers.

© M. L. Thomas

© Robert Visser

"Rowing: a competitive sport of boats that are narrow."

Great Soviet Encyclopaedia

© Brian Hill

of as a tiller at the stern. The cox steered the rudder post with his hand or could even use his knees if necessary.

Pocock oars were formed from two hollow shells around a solid center, joining four pieces of wood from British Columbia for the keels and gunwales of his boats. He claimed that pound for pound, this wood was "tougher than steel." He managed to locate an even harder wood, Australian ironbark, for the seat roller track. The seats themselves were made of Idaho white pine. For the skin of the boat, Pocock chose red cedar, stretched over 59 pairs of ribs of Indiana ash. Rudders were made of wild cherry or Honduras mahogany. The result was a great gourmet meal of a boat, with every detail finely crafted, every choice made to enhance the performance of the vehicle, and every part put together to please esthetically. Small wonder that oarspeople still smile at the sight of an Pocock shell. A

heavyweight crew could race at up to 15 miles (twenty-four kilometers) per hour in one of these beauties.

In order to explain how George Pocock came to Washington to become America's premier boatbuilder, a small digression is necessary to introduce another extraordinary man, Coach Hiram Conibear. Conibear was a lowly assistant coach for the Chicago White Sox baseball team when a job opened up for a football coach at the University of Washington in 1906. When he landed the position, Conibear did not know that Washington had a rowing crew, nor did he care, as he had never lifted an oar in his life. When he arrived, he found himself proposed for crew coach instead of football. He complained, "I don't know one end of the boat from another," and he was duly directed to the college library, to find books to read on the subject.

*THE BRIGHTLY COLORED OARS (LEFT)
are a symbol of the pageantry and tradition that
surrounds the sport of rowing, and accompanies
the rower through every race. Though his first
allegience is to the team, any crew member also
feels responsibility to win for all those before him
who rowed under these colors. Today, oars are
made from fiberglass and carbon fiber. This
construction cuts two pounds from the weight of
the oar, though it also sacrifices some of the lovely
craftsmanship of the old wooden shafts (below).*

THE QUEST FOR A BETTER OAR

*I*F ANY OARMAKER HAS CONTINUED THE PO-
*cock philosophy of innovating with the best materials, it has been
the firm of the Dreissigacker brothers of Morrisville, Vermont.
Dreissigacker means "thirty acres" in German, probably some
farmer's boast years ago about how much land he owned. Nowadays
the Dreissigackers are more preoccupied with water than land. They
noticed that despite all the synthetic shells being produced, most rowers
used old wooden oars, for lack of a replacement. The wood chipped,
cracked, and fell apart after use and neglect. After planning and
design in the Pocock-Conibear tradition, the Dreissigackers came up
with a model. The brothers' oar is built of a blade of light plastic foam
strong carbon fiber, and durable fiberglass. The shaft, likewise,
consists of fiberglass and carbon fiber. The handle is of basswood, and
the sleeves of plastic.*

*Yale coach Tony Johnson tested the product and discovered that
each of the Dreissigacker's oars weighed two pounds less than the
wooden nine-pounder. The result: sixteen pounds (7.2 kilograms)
saved in boat weight, more than could be gained by beheading the
coxswain. Johnson ordered a shipment of the Dreissigacker oars, and
other crews were quick to follow suit. Yale used the devices in the 1978
Eastern Sprints and beat Harvard. Orders rolled in even quicker.
Now the brothers sell over 200 oars per month and have expanded
their operations. Rowers have discovered that with the Dreissigacker
oar, a different balance occurs and they carry less weight in the hand,
a welcome sensation. Getting the blade out of the water is easier too, or
at least it seems easier, which amounts to the same thing. Dreissigacker oars are here to stay.*

Faintly as tolls the evening chime,
Our voices keep tune and our oars keep
time.
From Poems Relating to America,
Thomas Moore

© M. L. Thomas

© M. L. Thomas

And all the way, to guide their chime,
With falling oars they kept the time.
From Bermudas, *Andrew Marvell*

SO WE BEAT ON, BOATS AGAINST THE current, borne back ceaselessly into the past.

From **The Great Gatsby,** *F. Scott Fitzgerald*

© Bruce Hands

Conibear was open to reconsider rowing technique and equipment from the ground up, because he had no preconceived notions about tradition. First, this tobacco-spitter from the White Sox had to teach himself a foreign vocabulary of athletic movement. Armed with a megaphone, he screamed curses at the crew, borrowing from the vocabulary of Ty Cobb and other baseball ruffians. One of the athlete's parents complained to the college administration about this coach who not only screamed obscenities at the youths, but taught them what they had already read in the college library. Conibear excused his language this way: "I have to yell and cuss a little in order to bluff my way along until I have a chance to grasp what I'm trying to coach." While stalling for time, he made off with a skeleton from the biology lab and fixed it in a rowing seat at home, to figure out the physiology of the sport.

With this mad-scientist approach, Conibear soon had notions to contribute. He came up with a different stroke, a comfortable movement that did not strain the stomach and legs. At the same time, Conibear calculated with pen and paper how to improve the balance of boats. Some were so narrow and "cranky" that in order to keep balanced, "men had to part their hair in the middle and divide chewing tobacco evenly between their cheeks," one rower claimed. Conibear brought George Pocock from Vancouver and began a working relationship that proved highly productive.

Conibear was relentless in his fundraising efforts. Pocock had to be supported and kept busy with orders. So the Coach threatened alumni that if the shells could not materialize due to lack of money,

"the blame will fall on miserly, narrowminded persons like yourselves." In Washington, this approach was oddly successful.

Conibear had found a soul-mate in Pocock, who was willing to go to endless pains to achieve the shell of Conibear's dreams. These two perfectionists would have been dissatisfied working with anyone less dedicated to their common goals.

With America's entrance into World War I in 1917, international competitions ceased, but the reputation of the Pocock shell had already been established through the widespread influence of Conibear's approaches. The Coach himself did not survive long to savor his triumph. In 1917 he fell out of a fruit tree in his backyard and died of a broken neck, leaving behind a distinguished legacy.

After Conibear's death, his innovations continued to grow in popularity. His successor at Washington, Ed Leader, left to coach Yale in 1922, bringing Richard Pocock, George's son, with him. He had learned from Conibear that, no matter how great the coach's notions of design, a Pocock was essential for success.

As generations went by, new, faster fiberglass boats were introduced, which tended to be cheaper than wood because they are more easily produced. They are also easier to maintain.

There is also the factor of speed involved in the choice of a fiberglass shell. Speed demons will always choose fiberglass over wood. Yet the beauty of a wooden boat attracts devotees. Unlike racers, recreational rowers need not worry about finishing first. They can adopt the Sanskrit proverb, as restated by Leonard Woolf, "It's the journey, not the arrival, that matters."

CHAPTER TEN

INDOOR ALTER- NATIVES

L IKE ANY OTHER RITUAL ACT OF GRACE AND beauty, rowing requires a certain amount of formal preparation. To strengthen the body for the sport when outdoor weather is ominous, rowers developed a battery of indoor exercises. Harvard's crew exercise their legs and lungs by "doing stadiums," running up and down thirty-seven aisles of the Harvard Football stadium without a pause. The athletes have wryly termed this practice a "tour de stade," as if the French words give a degree of class to a bunch of sweaty jocks running their legs off. The term "doing stadiums" itself is a take-off on the Yale custom of "doing stairs." This means running up and down a dozen flights of steps at Yale's Payne Whitney gymnasium, a gothic grey stone edifice that would make a good set for a Dracula film.

College gyms are odd buildings, redolent of dank, fetid odors, full of eerie silences punctuated by abrupt noises. Nerves of steel are required to descend to the sub-basements where the still water rowing tanks are kept. These tubs of water, far from drinking quality, float practice boats that rowers use when the vagaries of weather keep them off the rivers. Mirror-lined walls permit self-study of technique and a sense that someone is watching.

AMID DISORIENTING echoes and splashes of fetid water, these rowers are trying to stay in shape through the winter by using an indoor rowing tank. Some athletes manage a mind-over-matter transcendence of their less-than-ideal surroundings, but what a shock awaits them after the workout, when they place a tentative foot on what should be a wooden dock and find that they are instead stepping on cold cement!

© Brian Hill

© Robert Visser

A typical workout for a crew in the tanks is an all-out effort in intervals of decreasing time. A piece of ten minutes may be followed by one of eight minutes, and so on. Without the psychological edge of actual competition, it does a rower's heart good to know that the next bit of torture will be briefer than the previous one.

After the tanks, a group might do "stairs" or "stadiums," and then break for lunch. Weight circuits are scheduled for the afternoon. When Tiff Wood was training for competition, his group went through a six-station weight course five times, with fifty repetitions at each stop. Sit-ups, bench rows, clean lifts, a rowing back-exercise machine, Nautilus leg extensions, and Nautilus hamstring exercises were all on the menu. The "clean" is a renowned weightlifting motion, which has been called a vertical version of the rowing stroke. An amusing photo exists of ex-fighter and crew coach Karl Adam

showing how a "clean" is done with a huge barbell. The earnest expression on the coach's face and his strain for perfect form despite a portly build, will strike a chord in the heart of every rower. Along with the "clean," rowers usually endure a "bench pull." They lie face-down on a narrow bench, take a barbell at the full extension of their arms, and bring the bar towards them, pulling the elbows into the body. Strength and endurance are the key goals of these two lifts. Upright rows, bent-over rows, and squat thrusts are terms most people hope they will never know the exact meaning of.

Rowing machines have many advantages, not the least of which is that they are operated indoors. Oddly, the machines were not always designed for indoor use. The first rowing machine appears to have been the Road Sculler of the 1890s. It was sort of a go-cart, propelled by an oarsman with pulleys connected to large tricycle wheels. The Road Sculler looks as incongruous as a bathtub taken for a drive in the country, yet appeared in road races and "go as you please" races in the old Madison Square Garden.

Perhaps unfortunately, all of today's rowing machines are stationary. Their technical name is rowing ergometer, which means a device measuring force. Everyone's favorite ergometer is the Concept II, which calibrates energy output more precisely than anyone would ever want to know. More important, it duplicates most closely the "feel" of being on the water. The rower pulls on a flywheel that spins around with adjustable resistance. The slide-seat format is like that of a racing boat. In short, the rowing ergometer can build strength as well as any exercise save rowing itself.

Athletes react differently to the machine. Steve Kiesling has written that the mere sound of the ratcheting wheels of the older

© Robert Visser

models is an efficient laxative. Other rowers grow fond of the machines that point an accusing needle at their degrees of fitness and remind them of gruelling courses on the water.

Tiff Wood, an enthusiast, founded the first annual Indoor Rowing Championships, called CRASH-B for "Charles River Association of Sculling Has-Beens." Every February, sculling has-beens, never-wases, and, current champions compete for the best time in a 2500 meter run. There are heats and finals for men and women, light- and heavyweights of all ages. Official records are kept by timers who sit next to each ergometer. In 1987, the entrants numbered over 700, representing numerous countries including the Soviet Union, and spectators filled the stands. Yet CRASH-B maintains a flavor all its own from its earlier and less formal days. A special trophy called "fly and die" is awarded to the rower with the fastest first mile, and a solo violinist plays an off-key version of the Star-Spangled Banner. "Commodore" Tiff Wood presides with all the dignity appropriate to the endeavor. Among the official paraphernalia are flags, official jackets, and rules on starting.

Not all ergometer users, however, are after pleasure: some are after pain. John Biglow uses the exercise machines all year round to "tune his pain receptors." By working his muscles until they lack oxygen, Biglow starts to hurt. He keeps lifting weights until he is exhausted. Then he goes outdoors to row. By doing so, Biglow aims at creating a "situation where my muscles have to find the smoothest, easiest way to row." This rigorous workout prepares him for the final sprint of actual races, when exhaustion inevitably sets in. His other goal is to work his muscles "as hard as I work them on the weight machines" whenever he rows. He matches the pain he feels on the exercise machines with the experience of pushing his endurance to the limit in a boat.

With ergometer races, as with almost all things in rowing, the British preceded the Americans. A clipping from an unidentified newspaper dated July 7, 1952 shows a photo of the "Dry Land Rowing Championship of the British Empire." A team called the Lord's Taverner Eight Damp Bobs, a group of elderly mustachioed men, are shown sitting in what looks like a hog-feeding trough alongside a combined Oxbridge crew incapacitated by laughter. In the background, the audience, in black tie and tails, watches this extravaganza with dignity. The photo caption explains that the racers sat in shells designed and built by Eton Masters and students (explaining the high-school wood-shop appearance of the vehicles) and the impact of the crews' pulling was "registered by colored liquid rising in two thermometer glass tubes the height of the ballroom." The originator of this competition was the Marshal of the Royal Air Force, Lord Tedder and proceeds went to charity. Only the Yanks, however, would make this freakish example of British wit into an annual event.

ANDY SUDDUTH (WORKING OUT ON THE NAUTILUS AND IN front of the mirror on the previous pages) is a firm believer in sufficient practice all year round. His determination and single-mindedness is similar to that of the brother of Stuart Little in E.B. White's children's classic. When Stuart is lost, his brother searches in the cellar but is distracted by an "old discarded rowing machine." For Sudduth, too, there is no more important task than a workout on the rowing machine.

THIS COULD BE THE PRECURSOR TO THE CRASH-B ERGOMEter Sprints. Or it could be an example of the rather mean conditions that rowers were made to endure in earlier rowing times. No doubt, this 1910 Columbia Squad was fed a meal of half-cooked meat and bread crumbs after their sweatshop workout.

EPILOGUE

I N 1907, AN EARLY PSYCHOANALYST, DR. GOTT-lob Spee, published a learned treatise on the motivation of the oarsman, the title of which is translated from the German as *Observations and Reflections on the Art and Skill of Rowing*. The doctor's ideas are as ponderous as his title. Spee found that an erotic undertone was inescapable in the sport. After all, didn't the athlete grip an impressively outsized phallic symbol, or even two of them? Didn't he perpetually dip these *phalloi* into the water, symbol of the eternally feminine? However, the good doctor did not stop with *eros*. He also found an inescapable religious element in the sport. Rowers often bear wounds on their palms, "like some of the more popular Italian saints," commented Dr. Spee. Furthermore, they put up with boils and other physical discomforts that would "try the patience of Job."

So, psychoanalytic images of the rower depict him either as an erotomaniac or as a saintly masochist. There may be some truth to both of these views, for rowing, like any sport that pushes people to their physical limits, attracts its share of masochists. The English poet,

Algernon Charles Swinburne, a renowned flagellant, was said to have joined his prep school rowing team only because the coach was reputed to apply a whip to the backs of laggards. Swinburne found soon enough that his hopes of whippings would not be realized, so he abandoned the sport for rugby, where at least some physical punishment was guaranteed.

However, people are drawn to rowing for a wide variety of reasons. Loners relish the experience of solitary sculling. Social animals enjoy the synchronicity demanded of a crew. Those who cannot stand to be alone are fulfilled by working out and competing with numerous other people during the course of the rowing season. Rowing can afford both solitude and companionship, competition and solo efforts. It fulfills the old and young, the superfit and the handicapped, men and women, and even children.

The rower's attraction to the water is understandable even without the womb imagery that Dr. Spee called upon. No matter how polluted a river, it still seems less tainted than concrete. Despite motorboats that roar past, leaving noise and waves in their wake, there is an irrevocable sense of the raw challenge of nature, a feeling of "us against the world," to rowing.

Most of the independent-minded people profiled in this book have not felt the need to analyse their love of rowing. Their instinct is not to chew over the reasons why they enjoy the exertions of the sport. A rower's response to challenges, worries, any of life's travails is "when in doubt, row!"

APPENDIX ONE:
ANNOTATED BIBLIOGRAPHY

Ackermann-Blount, Joan. "These Geers are in Overdrive." *Sports Illustrated*, v. 56, Feb 22, 1982, p. 28.
Lively portrait of the sisters from Vermont, Judy and Carlie Geer, who row well together and separately. Ignore the pun in the title.

The Annual Register, London, 1775 (Friday June, 23).
Edition commemorating the Venetian Regatta that was staged in London.

Bauer, Seth. "Coxing an Eight," *Ultrasport*, September 1986, p. 50.
Three-time World Championship cox Bauer explains what it feels like to be in charge of a crew. Like Bauer himself—short but able.

Bauer, Seth. "The Mechanics." *Ultrasport*, March/April 1985.
Gives the lowdown on Kris Korzeniowski, the latest coaching sensation from Poland who has taken control of the U.S. Olympic team.

Bourne, Gilbert C. *Memories of an Eton Wet-Bob of the Seventies*. London: Oxford University Press, 1933.
A comparative physiologist looks back to his early rowing days, with wry wit and good sense.

Burnell, R.D. *A Short History of the Leander Club, 1818 to 1968*. Henley-on-Thames, Oxon: Leander Club Publishers, 1968.
Erudite rowing Scholar's brief, anecdotal memoir.

Cassidy, Anne. "The Comeback of Dolly D." *McCalls*, Nov. 1983, p. 51.
The story of Dolly Driscoll, the former Radcliffe oarswoman who returned to rowing despite physical disabilities.

Cleaver, Hylton. *A History of Rowing*. London: Herbert Jenkins, 1957.
British rowing only, dealt with in a sniffy style.

Cohen, Scott. *Jocks*. New York: Pantheon, 1983.
Fanzine narrative, but notable for interview with Steve Kiesling.

Cook, Thomas. *Thos. Doggett Deceased: A Famous Comedian*. London: Constable, 1908.
Evocative picture of 18th century London in this biography of the founder of the famous Coat and Badge Race, held annually on the Thames.

Dangell, Sydney. *Odes and Idylls*. London: Macmillan, 1874.
No one will pick up this book today, but at its time it might have been popular.

Dodd, Christopher. *The Oxford and Cambridge Boat Race*. London: Stanley Paul, 1983.
Fully documented grab-bag of articles on various aspects of the Race.

Encyclopedia Britannica, 14th ed., "Rowing," by Keith L. Osborne.
Notwithstanding the general overall decline of this reference work, an able, helpful historical article mentioning many names.

Fairbairn, Ian, ed. *Steve Fairbairn on Rowing*. London: Nicholas Kaye, 1951.
The great coach from Cambridge speaks out in many different guidebooks reprinted here; valuable though repetitive.

Goodrich, Llyod. *Thomas Eakins*. Cambridge: Harvard University Press, 1982.
Decent reproductions of many works by the greatest modern artist of the sport, a study that is well-documented if not psychologically acute.

Haig-Thomas, David. *I Leap Before I Look*. New York: Putnam, 1936.
Dilettante sportsman looks back on rowing, among other things.

Halberstam, David. *The Amateurs*. New York: William Morrow, 1985.
Journalistic effort that has received widespread attention due to the author's renown in the fields of criticizing politics and industry.

Hall-Craggs, J.F. *The History of the Lady Margaret Boat Club*. Vol. II: *St. Johns College, Cambridge, 1929-1956*. Cambridge University Press for the Johnian Society, 1957.
For those who wish to plow through this scholarly work, it is a source for a surprising number of scabrous anecdotes.

Harrison, Mrs. Burton N. "Sweet Bells Out of Tune." *Century*, April 1893.
A concerned mother guesses her son's thoughts before and during a turn-of-the-century race between Harvard and Yale.

Heiland, Louis. *Undine Barge Club, Philadelphia*, Philadelphia: Fell Publishers, 1925.
Reflects considerable devotion to this old organization on the Schuylkill River in Philadelphia.

Howard, Ronnie, and Nigel Hunt. *Knowing Rowing*. South Brunswick and New York: A.S. Barnes and Co, 1977.
How-to book by experienced British coach, notable for the endless number of photos of the staggeringly handsome oarsman Hunt.

Hughes, Thomas. *Memoir of a Brother*. London: Macmillan, 1874.
The author of Tom Brown's Schooldays, *a Victorian bestseller, pays tribute to his brother, a rower who died prematurely.*

Keller, Thomi. "Notes on the Future of Rowing." *American Rowing*, January/February 1987, p. 28.
Fierce Swiss head of the FISA sets a crowd straight in Topeka, Kansas, and make no mistake about it!

Kelley, Robert. *American Rowing: Its Backgrounds and Traditions*. New York: G.P. Putnam's Sons, 1932.
Good on historical stuff, including a funny photo of a "land sculler," a sort of oarsman's tricycle.

Kiesling, Stephen. "Connoisseurs of Pain." *American Health*, November-December 1983, p. 62.
The author of The Shell Game *looks at how his old roommate John Biglow and sculler Ginny Gilder deal with bodily ills.*

Kiesling, Stephen. *The Shell Game*. New York: William Morrow 1982.
From the Yale-Harvard race to Henley and back, a college oarsman's narrative: good starting point for readers on the sport.

Kirch, Barbara. *Row For Your Life: A Complete Program Of Aerobic Endurance Training*. NY: Simon and Schuster, 1985.
Useful, no-frills guide to getting down and doing it, particularly good for handicapped rowers.

Lambert, Craig. "The Older We Get, the Better We Were." *Ultrasport*, September 1986, p. 43.
The phenomenon of Master's Races, where competitive rowing is enjoyed by those aged 50 and over.

Lehmann R.C. *Anni Fugaces: A Book of Verse with Cambridge Interludes*. London: John Lane, The Bodley Head, 1901.
Amusing doggerel; a lot exists of much less quality.

Lenk, Hans, ed. *Handlungsmuster Leistungssport: Karl Adam zum Gedenken*. Schorndorf: Hofmann, 1977.
Don't worry, it only means, in essence, "We're thinking of you, Karl," a tribute and in part, a memoir about coach Adam.

Lewis, Arthur H. *Those Philadelphia Kellys*. New York: William Morrow, 1977.
One of the earlier books that dissects the family problems of the Kellys of rowing and Hollywood fame.

Maclaren, Archibald. *Training in Theory and Practice*. London: Macmillan, 1866.
Unsentimental Oxford trainer offers advice that still makes good sense today.

MacOrlan, Pierre. *Images sur la Tamise*. Paris: Nouvelle Revue Francaise, 1925.
That's Thames to many; A Frog's-eye view of the Boat Race and other matters incomprehensibly English.

Mendenhall, Thomas C. *A Short History of American Rowing*. Boston: Charles River Books, 1981.
Reliable, dutiful history, with pages of statistics of many races. From the point of view of data on rowing, Mendenhall is the dean.

Moore, Marianne. *Collected Prose*. New York: Viking 1987.
Unfortunately no poems on rowing, but a good pleading letter to save a Brooklyn boathouse is included here.

Nickalls, Gully. *A Rainbow in the Sky: Reminiscences by G.O. (Gully) Nickalls*. London: Chatto and Windus, 1974.
Diverting memoirs by the son of Guy Nickalls, a rowing personality in his own right.

Nickalls, Guy. *Life's a Pudding*. London: Faber, 1939.
The legendary sculler has his say, and eloquently, too.

Nickalls, Major Vivian. *Oars, Wars and Horses*. London: Hurst and Blackett, 1932.
Guy's brother speaks for himself, not without a certain swagger.

Parker, Harry. "1979 Harvard-Yale Boat Race." *American Rowing*, March/April 1987, p. 22.
The stiff-upper lip Harvard coach lets down his guard to root for an exciting Race in the memory sweepstakes.

Pileggi, Sarah. "Ginny Gilder." *Sports Illustrated*, v. 60, June 25, 1984, p. 86.
Description of the sculler Gilder, with some thoughts on training and competition.

Raymond, Peter. "The Revenge of the Hammer." *Ultrasport*, January/February 1984, p. 40.
U.S. sculler Tiff Wood is profiled in an appealing tongue-in-cheek manner.

Robbart, Ann M. "Chris Ernst." *American Rowing*, January/February 1987, p. 10.
Talk with a fascinatingly frank and outspoken team player.

Rolfe, Fred. *The Venice Letters*. London: Cecil and Amelia Woolf Publishers, 1974.
The author of Hadrian VII *wrote these admiring letters to a British patron about coxswains and others he met in Venice around 1910.*

Rubin, Reed. "Rubin on Rowing." *The Oxford Magazine*, vol. LXXVII, no. 2, October 23, 1958, p. 22.
After losing the Boat Race with them, the American rower Rubin gives the Oxford crew what-for in a civilized manner.

Schaelchlin, Patricia A. *The Little Clubhouse on Steamship Wharf: San Diego Rowing Club 1888-1983*. Leucadia, California: Rand Editions, 1984.
Social history of American slang and recreational habits over the century.

Spee, Gottlob. *Observations and Reflections on the Art and Skill of Rowing*. New York: Cambridge University Press, 1909.
A legendary figure in the early development of psychoanalysis, held up by some in ridicule of the realities of Sigmund Freud.

Topolski, Daniel. *Boat Race: The Oxford Revival*. London: Willow Books, 1985.
Profane and quirky view of the Oxford-Cambridge rivalry as narrated by a veteran coach.

Ulbrickson, Al. "Rockne of Rowing." *Saturday Evening Post*, June 19, 1937, p. 14.
Although many coaches might like to think they've earned this title, the present article is about Washington's Hiram Conibear, trail-blazer.

Wallechensky, David. *The Complete Book of the Olympics*, New York: Viking, 1985.
Salt-peanuts-style trivia about Olympic rowing and other sports.

Ward, Irene. *The Ward Brothers: Champions of the World*. New York: Vantage Press, 1958.
A descendant of the famous U.S. competitive rowers, in a hagiographic life story.

Walker, Donald. *Manly Exercises*. London: John Lane, The Bodley Head, 1838.
Snobby comments about rowing et al, mainly notable for delicate Flaxman-style line drawings telling you how to row daintily.

Water Sports for the Disabled. London: EP Publishing, 1983.
Excellent, useful guide, well-illustrated and comprehensive.

Winter, Gordon. "Rowing Prints for the Collector." *Apollo*, v. 25, April 1937, p. 187.
This article may have sparked the intense competition between collectors Tom Mendenhall and Donald Beer for memorabilia.

Woodgate, W.B. *Reminiscences of an Old Sportsman*. London: Eveleigh Nash, 1909.
Details exactly why the author was known to friends as "Guts."

SCHEDULE

March

Tom White Invitational, Oak Ridge, Tennessee

The Heart of Texas, Austin, Texas

The Tennessee Cup, Oak Ridge, Tennessee

Spring Head of the Snohomish, Everett, Washington

Miami International Rowing Regatta, Key Biscayne, Florida

Philadelphia Scholastic Rowing Association Regatta, Philadelphia, Pennsylvania

San Diego Rowing Club Spring Regatta, San Diego, California

Annual Fawley Cup Regatta, Spokane, Washington

Green Lake Spring Regatta, Seattle, Washington

April

San Diego Lowenbrau Crew Classic, San Diego, California

Augusta Invitational Regatta, Augusta, Georgia

April Fool's Race, Norwich, Connecticut

Occoquan Invitational College Regatta, Lorton, Virginia

Husky Invitational, Seattle, Washington

Cherry Blossom Regatta, Alexandria, Virginia

Corvallis Invitational, Corvallis, Oregon

Orange Cup (Northeastern-Syracuse-Penn), Syracuse, New York

Keuper's Cup Regatta, Melbourne, Florida

George Mason Regatta, Lorton, Virginia

President's Regatta, Topeka, Kansas

Daffodil Invitational, Tacoma, Washington

Philadelphia Scholastic Rowing Association Regatta, Philadelphia, Pennsylvania

Washburn Open President's Regatta, Topeka, Kansas

Governor's Cup Regatta, Melbourne, Florida

Portland Regatta, Portland, Oregon

Atlanta Cup Regatta, Atlanta, Georgia

Annual West Virginia Governor's Cup Regatta, Charleston, West Virginia

Stanford Classic Redwood Shores Regatta, Stanford, California

San Diego City Rowing Championships, San Diego, California

U.T. Bradley Cup, Winter Park, Florida

Florida Intercollegiate Rowing Association Championships, Tampa, Florida

Blackwell Cup (Columbia-Penn-Yale), New York, New York

Smith Cup (Smith-Northeastern-Boston University-MIT-UNH), Boston, Massachusetts

Sunflower State Championships, Topeka, Kansas

The 2000 Grand, Grand Rapids, Michigan

Mercyhurst Invitational, Erie, Pennsylvania

Tri-Cities Regatta, Tricities, Washington

Meyer Cup Regatta, Tacoma, Washington

Minnesota Collegiate Rowing Championships, Minneapolis, Minnesota

Lake Merritt Sprints, Oakland, California

SIRA, Oak Ridge, Tennessee

Opening Day Regatta, Seattle, Washington

President's Cup Regatta, Poughkeepsie, New York

Midwest Sprint Championships, Madison, Wisconsin

Southwest Regionals, Long Beach Marina, California

May

Dogwood Regatta, Oak Ridge, Tennessee

Northern Virginia Scholastic Rowing Association, Occoquan, Virginia

Cincinnati Viking Cup, Cincinnati, Ohio

Philadelphia Scholastic Rowing Association Regatta, Philadelphia, Pennsylvania

New England Invitational Championships, Worcester, Massachusetts

South Oregon Open Regatta, Klamath Falls, Oregon

Eastern Sprints, Boston, Massachusetts

Port Promenade, San Francisco, California

Dad Vail Regatta, Philadelphia, California

Toledo Regatta, Toledo, Ohio

Alcatraz Island, San Francisco, California

Northwest Regional Championships, Seattle, Washington

EARC Sprints Regatta, Worcester, Massachusetts

International Regatta at Toledo, Toledo, Ohio

Small Boat Races, Newport, Rhode Island

Oakland Cup, San Francisco, California

Mayor's Cup, Providence, Rhode Island

Riverside Sprints, Cambridge, Massachusetts

Pacific Coast Rowing Championships, Sacramento, California

Memorial Day Regatta, St. Paul, Minnesota

Dragon Boat Regatta, Philadelphia, Pennsylvania

June

Regatta on Hammon Lake, Tioga, Pennsylvania

Cincinnati Invitational Regatta, Cincinnati, Ohio

Tulsa's Green Country Regatta, Tulsa, Oklahoma

"FESI"VAL Regatta, Lowell, Massachusetts

Rose Arts Race, Norwich, Connecticut

Schuylkill Navy Regatta, Philadelphia, Pennsylvania

US Rowing National Championships, Indianapolis, Indiana

Annual North Tahoe Rowing Regatta, King's Beach, California

Badger State Games, Madison, Wisconsin

Charm City Sprints, Baltimore, Maryland

Derby Sweep & Sculls, Derby, Connecticut

July

Empire State Games Trials, Buffalo, New York

Annual Hanmer Boat Races, Saranac Lake, New York

Moby Dick Classic, New Bedford, Massachusetts

4th of July Race, Benicia, California

Independence Day Regatta, Philadelphia, Pennsylvania

Fire Cracker 12. Norwich, Connecticut

Somes Sound Rowing Classic, Southwest Harbor, Maine

West Side Rowing Club Masters Championships, Buffalo, New York

The State Games of Oregon, Hillsboro, Oregon

Celebration of Henley, Marina Del Rey, California

West Side Rowing Club Invitational, Buffalo, New York

The Grand Regatta, Grand Rapids, Michigan

Lake Merritt Whaleboat Sprints, Oakland, California

Annual Alden Regatta, Toledo, Ohio

Chicago Spring Regatta, Chicago, Illinois

Annual Isles of Shoals Race, Kittery Point, Maine

Northwest Master's Regional Championships, Seattle, Washington

American Rowing Championships (Club Championships), Philadelphia, Pennsylvania

Sweeps and Sculls Regatta, Providence, Rhode Island

Blackburn Challenge, Gloucester, Massachusetts

Cromwell Cup Regatta, Cambridge, Massachusetts

Oak Ridge Sprints, Oak Ridge, Tennessee

August

Peconic Bay Round Robin, New Suffolk, New York

Norwalk River Regatta, Norwalk, Connecticut

Green Lake Summer Extravaganza, Seattle, Washington

Chicago's International Master's Regatta, Chicago, Illinois

Annual Northwestern International Rowing Association Championship Regatta, St. Paul, Minnesota

Firecracker Sprints 1500 Regatta, Nashua, New Hampshire

US Rowing Masters National Championships, Oak Ridge, Tennessee

Annual New Meadows River Cruise, Brunswick, Maine

Row for Life Regatta, Boston, Massachusetts

September

Inland Northwest Recreational Rowing Championships, Sandpoint, Idaho

FISA Master's World Championships, Strathclyde, Scotland

Harbor Day Race, Norwich, Connecticut

Bayada Regatta, Philadelphia, Pennsylvania

Providence Waterfront Festival Sprints, Providence, Rhode Island

Carnegie Lake Regatta, Princeton, New Jersey

Coast Guard Island Race, Oakland Estuary/San Francisco Bay, California

Annual Alden Ocean Shells Association Nationals, Schroon Lake, New York

Cedar River Regatta, Renton, Washington

Head of the Des Moines, Des Moines, Iowa

Head of the Hudson, Albany, New York

Head of the Ohio, Pittsburgh, Pennsylvania

Head of the Harbor, Boston, Massachusetts

King's Head II Regatta on the Schuylkill, King of Prussia, Pennsylvania

Gateway Regatta, St. Louis, Missouri

Sculler's Head of the Potomac Regatta, Washington, D.C.

Ship Shield Regatta, Burlington, New Jersey

Annual Sippican Ocean Rowing Regatta, East Marion, Massachusetts

Head of the Potomac, Alexandria, Virginia

October

Vallejo Whaleboat Regatta, Vallejo, California

Green Mountain Head Regatta, Putney, Vermont

Head of the Grand, Grand Rapids, Michigan

Textile River Regatta, Lowell, Massachusetts

Kearney Johnston Regatta, San Diego, California

Head of the Colorado, Austin, Texas

Head of the Mohawk River Regatta, Schenectady, New York

Head of the Merrimack Regatta, Nashua, New Hampshire

Ariel Regatta, Baltimore, Maryland

Head of the Connecticut River, Middletown, Connecticut

Head of the Erie Canal, Liverpool (Syracuse), New York

Head of the Rock, Rockford, Illinois

Chicago Iron Oars Marathon, Chicago, Illinois

Head of the Charles, Boston, Massachusetts

Annual Alden Ocean Shells Association Head Race on the Charles River, Boston, Massachusetts

Numerica's Cup Regatta, Manchester, New Hampshire

Head of the Schuylkill, Philadelphia, Pennsylvania

Head of the Spokane, Spokane, Washington

Head of the Milwaukee, Shorewood, Wisconsin

Hogan-Fries-Fontana Fall Invitational, Buffalo, New York

Head of the Occoquan, Springfield, Virginia

Head of the Tennessee Regatta, Knoxville, Tennessee

Tri-Mountain Regatta, Seattle, Washington

Jack Speakman Regatta, Columbus, Ohio

Head of the Fish Regatta, Saratoga Springs, New York

Head of the Estuary, Oakland, California

November

Head of the Chattahoochee Regatta, Atlanta, Georgia

Head of the Occoquan, Alexandria, Virginia

Head of the Snohomish, Everett, Washington

Falcon Fremont 4-Miler, Seattle, Washington

Head of the Dog, Portland, Oregon

Garden State Sprints, Mercer County, New Jersey

Green Lake Frostbite Regatta, Seattle, Washington

Head of the Licking, Cincinnati, Ohio

Head of the Lake, Seattle, Washington

Head of the Dragon Regatta, Indian Harbour Beach, Florida

Philadelphia Frostbite Regatta, Philadelphia, Pennsylvania

Bill Braxton Memorial Regatta, Philadelphia, Pennsylvania

APPENDIX THREE
ROWING CLUBS AND ORGANIZATIONS

Northeast

Alden Ocean Shell Assoc.
26 Plymouth Road
Port Washington, NY 11050

Alte Achter Boat Club
54 Creighton Street
Cambridge, MA 02140

American Sail Training Assoc.
365 Thames Street
Newport, RI 02840

Amherst College Rowing Assoc.
Alumni Gym
Amherst College
Amherst, MA 01002

Amoskeag Rowing Club
c/o YMCA
30 Mechanic Street
Manchester, NH 03101

Aqueduct Rowing Club, Inc.
2855 Aqueduct Road
Schenectady, NY 12309

Beer Belly Rowing Club
38 Terrace Avenue
Riverside, CT 06878

Belmont Rowing Assoc.
Club Bassett
350 Prospect Road
Belmont, MA 02178

Blood Street Sculls
151 Blood Street
Old Lyme, CT 06371

Boston "T" Club
275 Pearl Street
Braintree, MA 02184

Boston Rowing Club
PO Box 38
Cambridge, MA 02138

Brown Rowing Association
First Boston Corp.
Park Avenue Plaza
New York, NY 10055

Buckingham Browne & Nichols
Gerry's Landing Road
Cambridge, MA 02138

Cambridge Boat Club
Gerry's Landing Road
Cambridge, MA 02138

Cape Ann Rowing Club
PO Box 1715
Gloucester, MA 01931

Cascadilla Boat Club
Cornell University
Mary Donlon
106 Westfield Drive
Ithaca, NY 14853

Charles River Rowing Assoc.
60 J.F. Kennedy
Cambridge, MA 02138

Charter Oak Rowing Club
16 Sycamore Road
West Hartford, CT 06117

Chelsea Rowing Club
PO Box 22
Norwich, CT 06360

Community Rowing, Inc.
PO Box 2604
Boston, MA 02238

Community Rowing Program
275 Chestnut Street
Springfield, MA 01104

Connecticut Rowing & Boating
  Society
PO Box 1611
New London, CT 06320

Craftsbury Sculling Center
PO Box 31
Craftsbury Common, VT 05827

Dartmouth Rowing Club
301 Alumni Gym
Dartmouth College
Hanover, NH 03755

Durham Boat Club
RR #2
Durham, NH 03824

East Hampton Rowing Club
The Boat Shop
42 Gann Road
East Hampton, NY 11937

East Lyme Rowing Assoc., Inc.
PO Box 36
East Lyme, CT 06333

Eliot House Crew
19 Lakeview Road
Winchester, MA 01890

Empire State Rowing Assoc.
20 North Broadway
White Plains, NY 10601

Essex Rowing Club
PO Box 575
Ivoryton, CT 06442

Exeter Boat Club
Phillips Exeter Academy
Exeter, NH 03833

Florida Rowing Center, Inc.
1140 Fifth Avenue
New York, NY 10128

Gloucester Women's Rowing
53 Marmion Way
Rockport, MA 01966

Hanover Rowing Club
301 Alumni Gym
Dartmouth College
Hanover, NH 03755

Harbor Rowing Club
300 Congress
Boston, MA 02210

Hartford Barge Club
36 Country Lane
East Hampton, CT 06424

Head of the Connecticut F
353 Newfield Street
Middletown, CT 06457

Hobart & Wm. Smith Rc
PO Box SF93
Geneva, NY 14456

Housatonic Rowing Assoc.
574 Amity Road
Woodbridge, CT 06516

Hyde Park Rowing Assoc.
7 Howard Boulevard
Hyde Park, NY 12538

Independence Rowing Club
PO Box 1412
Nashua, NH 03061

Intercollegiate Rowing Assoc.
PO Box 3
Centerville, MA 02632

Interlachen Rowing Club
PO Box 330
Corning, NY 14830

Kings Crown Rowing Assoc.
PO Box 1263
Bowling Green Station
New York, NY 10274

Lake Placid Sports Council
Town Hall
Lake Placid, NY 12946

Litchfield Heights Rowing Club
PO Box 42
Litchfield, CT 06759

Little Brave Canoe Rowing Club
75 Mill Street
Randolph, MA 02368

Mercer City Boat Club
Box 991 Groton School
Groton, MA 01450

Merrimack River Rowing Assoc.
PO Box 686
Lowell, MA 01853

Merrymeeting Rowing Club
98 Maine Street
Brunswick, ME 04011

Middletown Rowing Assoc.
Middletown High School
Hunting Hill Avenue
Middletown, CT 06457

Mid-Hudson Rowing Assoc.
PO Box 683
Poughkeepsie, NY 12602

Narragansett Boat Club
PO Box 2413
Providence, RI 02906

N.E.I.R.A.
Phillips Academy
Andover, MA 01810

New Haven Rowing Club
44 Collier Circle
Hamden, CT 06518

New York Athletic Club
56 Prospect Avenue
Larchmont, NY 10538

Nonesuch Oar & Paddle Club
Prouts Neck
Scarborough, ME 04074

Norwalk River Rowing Club
3 Inwood Road
Norwalk, CT 06850

O.A.R.S.
53 South Ferry Street
Albany, NY 12202

Oars of Rhode Island
Tootell Center
University of Rhode Island
Kingston, RI 02881

Onota Lake Rowing Club
PO Box 411
Williamstown, MA 01267

Pioneer Valley Rowing Assoc.
Ferris Athletic Center
Trinity College
Hartford, CT 06106

Power 10 of New York
215 E. 72nd Street
New York, NY 10021

Riverside Boat Club
769 Memorial Drive
Cambridge, MA 02135

Rochester Rowing Club
41 Vick Park B
Rochester, NY 14607

Rockaway Rowing Club
69-49 De Costa Avenue
Arverne, NY 11692

Rude & Smooth Boat Club
46 East 91st Street
New York, NY 10028

Sagamore Rowing Assoc.
14 Windham Drive
Huntington Station, NY 11746

Saint Aubin Rowing Club
11 Hall Place
Exeter, NH 03833

Saratoga Springs Rowing Club
PO Box 1132
Saratoga Springs, NY 12866

Sebago Canoe Club
Foot of Avenue N
Brooklyn, NY 11236

Shimmo Rowing Club
237 Park Avenue
New York, NY 10017

Squamscott Scullers Inc.
PO Box 526
Exeter, NH 03833

Stonehill Rowing
112 Sheephill Road
Riverside, CT 06878

Syracuse Alumni Rowing Assoc.
PO Box 26
Lockport, NY 14094

Syracuse Chargers Rowing Club
4067 Ensign Drive
Liverpool, NY 13090

Syracuse University Crew
Manley Field House
Syracuse, NY 13244

Thames River Sculls
52 Vauxhall Street
New London, CT 06320

Union Boat Club
144 Chestnut Street
Boston, MA 02108

Vassar Rowing Club
Browning Road
Hyde Park, NY 12538

Warren Rowing Club
99 Hancock Street #10
Cambridge, MA 02139

Wavertree Life Rowing Assoc.
207 Front Street
New York, NY 10038

West Side Rowing Club
PO Box 506
Buffalo, NY 14213

Winsor Crew
Pilgrim Road
Boston, MA 02215

Worcester Rowing Assoc.
408 Whitney Street
Northboro, MA 01532

Yale Old Fellows Rowing Assoc.
RR 2, Box 130
Oneonta, NY 13820

1980 Rowing Club
22 Martins Lane
Hingham, MA 02043

Yankee Rowing Club
PO Box 408
North Amherst, MA 01059

Mid-Atlantic
Alexandria Crew Boosters
PO Box 3202
Alexandria, VA 22302

Allegheny River Rowing Club
206 Lehigh Avenue
Pittsburgh, PA 15232

American Express Rowing Assoc.
SE Cor. 16th & JFK
Philadelphia, PA 19102

American Rowing Assoc.
16 Aldwyn Lane
Villanova, PA 19085

The Annapolis Rowing Club
PO Box 4191
Annapolis, Maryland 21403

Bachelors Barge Club
116 E. Gorgas Lane
Philadelphia, PA 19119

Back Bay Viking Rowing Club
10 N. Iroquois Avenue
Margate City, NJ 08402

Baltimore Rowing Club
PO Box 10162
Baltimore, MD 21285

Bonner Rowing Assoc.
Landsdowne Avenue and Garrett
   Road
Drexel Hill, PA 19026

Brigantine Rowing Club
613 Woodland Avenue
Absecon, NJ 08201

Camden County Rowing Foundation
PO Box 1346
Camden, NJ 08105

Camsis Boat Club, Inc.
838 South 18th Street
Arlington, VA 22202

Carnegie Lake Rowing Assoc.
PO Box 3411
Princeton, NJ 08543

Chester River Rowing Club
104 South Cross Street
PO Box #180
Chestertown, MD 21620

Collegiate Rowing Assoc.
1812 Webster Lane
Ambler, PA 19002

Compote Rowing Assoc.
4068 Ridge Avenue
Philadelphia, PA 19129

Crescent Boat Club
#5 Boathouse Row
Philadelphia, PA 19130

Dad Vail Rowing Assoc.
1812 Webster Lane
Ambler, PA 19002

Fairfax Crew Assoc.
9525 Main Street
Fairfax, VA 22031

Fairmount Rowing Assoc.
335 W. State Street
Media, PA 19063

Father Judge Crew
5336 Saul Street
Philadelphia, PA 19124

Go Row Club
Suite 165
416 River Avenue
Williamsport, PA 17701

Lehigh Valley Rowing Assoc.
340 Cattell Street
Easton, Pa 18042

Malta Boat Club
59203 Delaire
Philadelphia, PA 19114

Mary Washington Crew Club
Box 3774 College Station
Fredericksburg, VA 22401

Mercy Hospital Foundation Crew
1515 Locust Street #700
Pittsburgh, PA 15219

Middle States Rowing Assoc.
2834 W. Clearfield Street
Malvern, PA 19355

Misery Bay Rowing Club
2504 Wayne Street
Erie, PA 16503

Monongahela Rowing Assoc.
PO Box 824
Morgantown, WV 26507

National Rowing Foundation
PO Box 6030
Arlington, VA 22206

Navesink River Rowing Club
PO Box 2297
Red Bank, NJ 07701

North Allegheny Rowing Team
10375 Perry Highway
Wexford, PA 15090

North Hills Rowing Club
5700 Corporate Drive
Pittsburgh, PA 15237

Northern Virginia Rowing Assoc.
PO Box 23042
Alexandria, VA 22304

Oak Leaf Center Rowing
4332 Montgomery Avenue
Bethseda, MD 20814

Occoquan Boat Club
PO Box 5493
Springfield, VA 22150

Ohio Valley Rowing Club
1800 Washington Avenue
Parkersburg, WV 26101

Old Dominion Boat Club
203 N. Ripley Street #303
Alexandria, VA 22304

Old Dominion Rowing Club
1123 Surrey Crescent
Norfolk, VA 23508

Oneida Boat Club Rowing Assoc.
York Street & River Front
Burlington, NJ 08016

Pennsylvania Athletic Club Rowing
   Assoc.
431 Newbold Road
Jenkintown, PA 19046

Philadelphia Frostbite Regatta
456 Militia Hill Road
Southampton, PA 18966

Potomac Boat Club
3530 Water Street NW
Washington, DC 20007

Potomac River Development Center
1517 N. Taylor Street
Arlington, VA 22207

Provident National Bank Rowing
   Assoc.
PO Box 7648
Philadelphia, PA 19101

Raritan Valley Rowing Assoc.
PO Box 1149
Piscataway, NJ 08855

Scholastic Rowing Assoc.
134 Sylvan Court
Alexandria, VA 22304

Susquehanna River Rowing
   Organization
Shamokin Dam, PA 17876

Susquehanna Rowing Assoc.
PO Box 2213
Harrisburg, PA 17101

Susquehanna University Crew Club
Susquehanna University
Selinsgrove, PA 17870

Triton Rowing Club
5 Summit Drive
Denville, NJ 07834

Undine Barge Club
730 Bryn Mawr Avenue
Narberth, PA 19072

United States Rowing Assoc.
2058 Poplar Street
Philadelphia, PA 19130

University Barge Club
7 Kelly Drive
Philadelphia, PA 19130

US Dragon Boat Assoc.
1812 Webster Lane
Ambler, PA 19002

Vesper Boat Club
10 East River Drive
Philadelphia, PA 19130

Viking Rowing Foundation
121 N. Oxford Avenue
Ventnor City, NJ 08406

Virginia Rowing Assoc.
Memorial Gym
Charlottesville, VA 22903

West Potomac Crew Boosters
PO Box 6211
Alexandria, VA 22306

Wilmington Rowing Club
PO Box 25248
Wilmington, DE 19899

Woodbridge Crew
PO Box 405
Occoquan, VA 22125

Woodrow Wilson Boosters
2724 36th Place NW
Washington, D.C. 20007

YMCA Three Rivers Rowing Assoc.
PO Box 23333
Pittsburgh, PA 15222

Southeast

Alumni Boat Club of Rollins College
2762 Sunbranch Drive
Orlando, FL 32822

American Barge Club, Inc.
Suite 400
Cedars West Bldg.
Miami, FL 33136

Atlanta Rowing Club, Inc.
145 Roswell Farms Circle
Roswell, GA 30075

Augusta Port Authority Rowing
Assoc.
PO Box 36
Augusta, GA 30903

Augusta Rowing Club
PO Box 36
Augusta, GA 30903

Biscayne Bay Rowing Assoc.
5801 SW 11th Street
Miami, FL 33144

Bulldog Rowing Club
701 Oxford
Houston, TX 77007

Charleston Rowing Club
University of Charleston
Charleston, WV 25304

The Citadel Crew
Dept. of Physical Ed.
Charleston, SC 29409

Dallas Rowing Club
PO Box 7309
Dallas, TX 75209

Florida Athletic Club
401 E. Tullis Avenue
Longwood, FL 32750

Gator Rowing Club
401 NW 34th Drive
Gainesville, Fl 32607

Harbor City Rowing Club
PO Box 2632
Melbourne, FL 32902

Inner City Marine Project
1450 NE 2nd Avenue
Room 907
Miami, FL 33132

Key West Maritime Historical
Society
RR 4, Box 902
Summerland Key, FL 33042

Knoxville Rowing Assoc.
PO Box 138
Knoxville, TN 37901

Lookout Rowing Club
120 Macfarland Avenue
Chattanooga, TN 37405

Louisville Rowing Club, Inc.
1611 Spring Drive 5E
Louisville, KY 40205

Miami Rowing Club
PO Box 49-0356
Key Biscayne, FL 33149

New Bern Boat Club
1706 River Drive
New Bern, NC 28560

Oak Ridge Rowing Assoc.
PO Box 240
Oak Ridge, TN 37831

Orlando Rowing Club
500 Rainbow Drive
Casselberry, FL 32707

Palm Beach Rowing Assoc.
301 Clematis Street
Suite 200
West Palm Beach, FL 33401

Palm Beach Rowing Club
1460 S. Ocean Boulevard
Lantana, FL 33462

Port Everglades Rowing Club
PO Box 30071
Fort Lauderdale, FL 33303

S.I.R.A.
2729 St. Augustine Trail
Marietta, GA 30067

St. John's Few Rowing Club
1176 Romaine Circle W
Jacksonville, FL 32225

Tampa Rowing Club
PO Box 22906
Tampa, FL 33622

Texas Recreational Rowing
PO Box 50424
Austin, TX 78763

Wolf River Rowing Club
44 N. Second Street 9th Fl
Memphis, TN 38103

Midwest

Austin Rowing Club
PO Box 1741
Austin, TX 78767

Buckeye Rowing Assoc.
4200 Royalton Road
Brecksville, OH 44141

Chicago River Aquatic Center
400 E. Randolph Street #2527
Chicago, IL 60601

Cincinnati Regatta
250 E. 5th Street
Cincinnati, OH 45202

Cincinnati Rowing Club
PO Box 20045
Cincinnati, OH 45220

Columbia Club Rowing Crew
121 Monument Circle
Indianapolis, IN 46204

Cuyahoga Rowing Assoc.
2520 Norfolk Road
Cleveland Heights, OH 44106

Des Moines Rowing Club
2300 Financial Center
Des Moines, IA 50309

Detroit Boat Club
Belle Isle
Detroit, MI 48207

Duluth Rowing Club
PO Box 655
Duluth, MN 55801

Ecorse Rowing Club
PO Box 4555
Detroit, MI 48204

Flint Rowing Club, Inc.
516 S. Grand Traverse Street
Flint, MI 48502

Grand Rapids Rowing Club
PO Box 3189
Grand Rapids, MI 49501

Grand Valley Rowing Club
9100 Victor
Jenison, MI 49428

Greater Columbus Rowing
1825 Victorian Court
Columbus, OH 43220

Illinois River Oarsmen
2207 Daycor Divide
Bartonville, IL 61607

Indianapolis Boat Club, Inc.
26 Southedge Drive
Brownsburg, IN 46112

Iowa Rowing Assoc.
Recreational Services
Field House
Iowa City, IA 52242

Lake Phalen Rowing Assoc.
1858 E. Shore Drive
Saint Paul, MN 55109

Lawrence Rowing Assoc.
333 Mississippi Street
Lawrence, KS 66044

Lincoln Park Boat Club
PO Box 146345
Chicago, IL 60614

Macomb-YMCA Rowing Program
36691 Jefferson
Mt. Clemens, MI 48045

Marietta Rowing Assoc.
Marietta College
Marietta, OH 45750

Mendota Rowing Club
2337 Monroe Street
Madison, WI 53711

Milwaukee Rowing Club
PO Box 11171
Milwaukee, WI 53211

Minneapolis Rowing Club
PO Box 6712
Minneapolis, MN 55406

Minnesota Boat Club
978 Hawthorne Avenue E
St. Paul, MN 55106

Oklahoma City Rowing Club
11712 Rocky Way
Warr Acres, OK 73162

Quad Cities Rowing Assoc., Inc.
2825 46th Street
Rock Island, IL 61201

Rockford YMCA Rowing
200 Y Boulevard
Rockford, IL 61107

St. Louis Rowing Club
PO Box 16292
St. Louis, MO 63105

Sooner Rowing Assoc.
4400 One Williams Center
Tulsa, OK 74172

Toledo Rowing Club
3600 N. Summit
Oregon, OH 43611

Topeka Rowing Assoc.
PO Box 2423
Topeka, KS 66601

Waterloo Rowing Club
PO Box 1435
Waterloo, IA 50704

Wyndotte Boat Club
14239 Stratford Street
Riverview, MI 48192

Northwest
Bend Metro Park & Recreational
   District
200 NW Pacific Park Lane
Bend, OR 97701

Central Oregon Rowing
NW College Way
Bend, OR 97701

Confluence Rowing Club
1327 11th Avenue
Lewiston, ID 83501

Conibear Rowing Assoc.
12105 NE 33rd Street
Bellevue, WA 98005

Everett Rowing Assoc.
3002 Wetmore Avenue
Everett, WA 98201

George Y Pocock Rowing
   Foundation
1014 10th Street
Snohomish, WA 98290

Great Falls Community Rowing
3419 6th Avenue N
Great Falls, MT 59401

Green Lake Crew
100 Dexter Avenue North
Seattle, WA 98109

Lake Ewauna Rowing Club
PO Box 1647
Klamath Falls, OR 97601

Lake Washington Rowing Club
PO Box 45117
University Station
Seattle, WA 98145

Lute Varsity Rowing Club
Athletic Dept. PLU
Tacoma, WA 98447

Mount Baker Rowing & Sailing
3800 Lake Washington Boulevard S.
Seattle, WA 98118

Oregon Assoc. of Rowers
4873 Old Dillard Road
Eugene, OR 97405

OIT Rowing Club
3201 Campus Drive
Klamath Falls, OR 97601

Portland Regatta Company
1300 SW 5th Avenue
Portland, OR 97201

Portland Rowing Club
PO Box 2370
Portland, OR 97202

Renton Rowing Assoc.
2109 Whitman Avenue NE
Renton, WA 98056

Salem Rowing Club
PO Box 482
Salem, OR 97308

Seattle Yacht Club Crew
1807 East Hamlin Street
Seattle, WA 98112

Station L Rowing Club
1724 SE 40th Avenue
Portland, OR 97214

Union Bay Rowing Club
Univ. of Washington
Sports Clubs GD-10
Seattle, WA 98195

Western Intercollegiate Rowing
   Assoc.
3414 3rd Avenue W.
Seattle, WA 98119

Whidbey Island Rowing Club
PO Box 370
200 NW Coveland Street
Coupville, WA 98239

Willamette Rowing Club
Frank Zagunis
55 SW Oriole Lane
Lake Oswego, OR 97034

Southwest

Balboa Yacht Club
1801 Bayside Drive
Corona Del Mar, CA 92625

Bay Area Whaleboat Rowing Assoc.
7 Harbor Way
Vallejo, CA 94590

Berkeley Crew Club
1880 San Ramon
Berkeley, CA 94707

Bulldog Rowing Club
36 Summit Avenue
Chatham, CA 07928

California Rowing Club
2759 Union Street
San Francisco, CA 94123

California Yacht Club
4469 Admiralty Way
Marina del Rey, CA 90292

Dolphin Swim & Boat Club
502 Jefferson Street
San Francisco, CA 94109

Don Row and the Rowmantics
155 Sansome, 9th floor
San Francisco, CA 94104

Head of the Harbor Regatta
USC Athletics
Los Angeles, CA 90089

Lake Merritt Rowing Club
PO Box 1046
Oakland, CA 94604

Long Beach Rowing Assoc.
PO Box 3879
Long Beach, CA 90803

Los Gatos Rowing Club
22025 Old Santa Cruz Highway
Los Gatos, CA 95030

Marin Rowing Assoc.
Ross, CA 94957

Mills Cyclone Crew
Haas Pavillion
Oakland, CA 94613

Mission Bay Rowing Assoc.
1001 Santa Clara Place
San Diego, CA 92109

Motley Rowing Club
4678 E. Banker Way
Long Beach, CA 90814

Newport Aquatic Center
PO Box 2417
Newport Beach, CA 92659

Newport Harbor Yacht Club
720 West Bay Avenue
Balboa, CA 92661

Northbay Rowing Club
124 Howard Street
Petaluma, CA 94952

Oakland Strokes
21 Maple Lane
Walnut Creek, CA 94595

Recreational Rowers
1470 Woodbridge Oak Way
Sacramento, CA 95833

Redwood Shores Stanford Class
#3 Twin Dolphin Drive #200
Redwood City, CA 94065

River City Rowing Club
2946 Bendmill Way
Sacramento, CA 95833

Rocky Mountain Rowing Club
PO Box 6242
Denver, CO 80206

San Diego Crew Classic
PO Box 6141
San Diego, CA 92106

San Diego Rowing Club
PO Box 2768
San Diego, CA 92112

San Francisco Police Academy
366 Mississippi Street
San Francisco, CA 94107

Santa Barbara Rowing Club
University of California Robertson
   Gym
Santa Barbara, CA 93106

Santa Cruz Rowing Club
PO Box 3164
Santa Cruz, CA 95063

Sausalito Rowing Club
PO Box 1657
Sausalito, CA 94966

Stockton Rowing Club
PO Box 2181
Stockton, CA 95201

The Dirty Dozen
2415 Mariner Square Drive
Alameda, CA 94501

Tahoe Rowing Club
PO Box 1835
Crystal Bay, NV 89402

TRW Rowing Assoc.
One Space Pike
Redondo Beach, CA 90278

Viking Crew of Long Beach
4901 E. Carson Street
Long Beach, CA 90808

ZLAC Rowing Club
1111 Pacific Beach Drive
San Diego, CA 92109

Rowing Schools

Craftsbury Sculling Camp
Craftsbury Center
PO Box 31
Craftsbury Common, VT 05827

Durham Boat Co., Inc.
RFD #2 Newmarket Rd.
Durham, NH 03824

Florida Rowing Center
13198 Forest Hill Boulevard
West Palm Beach, FL 33414

Florida Rowing School
Sandpiper Bay Resort
Port St. Lucie, FL 33452

Open Water Rowing Co.
133 Caznean Avenue
Sausalito, CA 94965

Rowing/NW
3304 Fuhrman Avenue E
Seattle, WA 98102

Small Boat Gallery
PO Box 156
George and Riggins Streets
Georgetown, MO 21930

Sparkhawk Sculling School
222 Porters Point Road
Colchester, VT 05446

Trent Sculling School
Lady Eaton College
Peterborough, Ont.
Canada K9J 7B8

Rowing for the Handicapped

Philadelphia Rowing Program for the
   Disabled
2601 Penn Avenue
Philadelphia, PA 19130

Freedom on the River Program
2567 Braiburn Circle
Ann Arbor, MI 48104

Mendota Rowing Club, Program for
   the Disabled
2305 Park Street
Madison, WI 53713

Lake Merritt Rowing Club
Program for the Disabled
P.O. Box 1046
Oakland, CA 94604

SOURCES

Equipment

Boats

Acoaxet Boat Co, Inc.
PO Box 506
Adamsville, RI 02801

Advance, USA
PO Box 452
East Haddam Industrial Park
East Haddam, CT 06423

Alcort Sailing Boats
South Leonard Street
Waterbury, CT 06725

Aeolus Boats
Old Coach Road
Davenport, CA 95017

Andreassen Boatworks
5619 Marine View Drive
Tacoma, WA 98422

Apple Line and Amsterdam Boat
    Works
146 Church Street
Amsterdam, NY 12010

Beachcomber Fiberglass Technology,
    Inc.
2850 SE Market Place
Stuart, FL 33497

Bill Knecht
PO Box 1346
Camden, NJ 08105

Laser International
1250 Tessier Street
Hawkesbury, Ont.
Canada K6A 1PS

Laser West
17935 Skypark Circle
Suite G
Irvine, CA 92714

Little River Marine
PO Box 986
Gainesville, FL 32602

Lowell's Boat Shop, Inc.
459 Main Street
Amesbury, MA 01913

Morley Cedar Canoes
PO Box 147
Swan Lake, MT 59911

North Pacific Marine
8926 Miller Road
Bainbridge Island, WA 98110

North River Boatworks
6 Elm Street
Albany, NY 12202

Omni-Cat Designs
11020 Solway School Road
Suite 103
Knoxville, TN 37931

Onion River Boatworks
Maple Street Box 4170
Waterbury Center, VT 05677

Owen Racing Shells
PO Box 1167
Sisters, OR 97759

Paluski Boats, Ltd.
RR3
Lakefield, Ont.
Canada K0L 2H0

Peinert Boatworks
52 Coffin Avenue
New Bedford, MA 02746

Seth Persson Boat Builders
18 Riverside Avenue
Old Saybrook, CT 06475

George Pocock Racing Shells, Inc.
509 NE Northlake Way
Seattle, WA 98105

Dietrich Rose
4068 Ridge Avenue
Philadelphia, PA 19129

RKL Boatworks
Pretty March Road
Mt Desert, ME 04660

Rowing Crafters
247 Gate 5 Road
Sausalito, CA 94965

Saroga
27 Hedly Street
Portsmouth, RI 02871

Shew and Burnham
PO Box 131
South Bristol, ME 04568

Shoenbrod Racing Shells
596 Elm Street
Biddeford, ME 04005

Stren Boats, Inc.
Box 653
Rockport, ME 04856

Small Craft, Inc.
59 Brunswick Avenue
Putnam, CT 06354

South Cove Boat Shop
PO Box 10
Montague, MA 01351

Steller Technology, Inc.
PO Box 4612
Middletown, RI 02840

Trout River Boatworks
Rt. 2, Box 304
Manitowish Waters, WI 54545

Vespoli USA, Inc.
385 Clinton Avenue
New Haven, CT 06513

Wing Systems
PO Box 568
Oyster Bay, NY 11771

Build-Your-Own
Boat Kits

Glen-L Marine Designs
9152 Rosecrans
Bellflower, CA 90706

Martin Marine Co.
Box 251
Goodwin Road
Kittery Pt, ME 03905

General Shell Corporation
Fairhaven
Foot of Spring Street
Sausalito, CA 94965

Woodenboat Magazine
PO Box 78
Brooklin, ME 04616

Sculling Oars Suppliers

Baltic Oar Co.
Box 766
Baltic, CT 06330

Concept II, Inc.
RR1, Box 1100
Morrisville, VT 05661

Durham Boat Co.
Ciolli
RFD#2, Newmarket Road
Durham, NH 03824

Onboard Products
459 Main Street
Amesbury, MA 01913

Plantedosi Oars, Inc.
PO Box 643 S
West Acton, MA 01720

Signature Oars
PO Box 795
Safety Harbor, FL 33572

INDEX